In the Fourth Year

ANTICIPATIONS OF A WORLD PEACE

BY

H. G. WELLS

AUTHOR OF "MR. BRITLING SEES IT THROUGH,"
"THE WAR AND THE FUTURE," "WHAT IS COMING?" "THE WAR THAT WILL
END WAR," "THE WORLD SET FREE," "IN THE DAYS OF
THE COMET," AND "A MODERN UTOPIA"

LONDON
CHATTO & WINDUS
1918

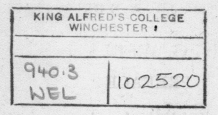

First published . . . *June 6, 1918*
Second Impression . . *June, 1918*

PRINTED IN ENGLAND BY WILLIAM CLOWES AND SONS, LIMITED,
LONDON AND BECCLES,

PREFACE

IN the latter half of 1914 a few of us were writing that this war was a " War of Ideas." A phrase, " The War to end War," got into circulation, amidst much sceptical comment. It was a phrase powerful enough to sway many men, essentially pacifists, towards taking an active part in the war against German imperialism, but it was a phrase whose chief content was its aspiration. People were already writing in those early days of disarmament and of the abolition of the armament industry throughout the world ; they realized fully the element of industrial belligerency behind the shining armour of imperialism, and they denounced the " Krupp-Kaiser " alliance. But against such writing and such thought we had to count, in those days, great and powerful realities. Even to those who expressed these ideas there lay visibly upon them the shadow of impracticability ; they were very " advanced " ideas in 1914, very Utopian. Against them was an unbroken mass of mental

habit and public tradition. While we talked of this
" war to end war," the diplomatists of the Powers
allied against Germany were busily spinning a
disastrous web of greedy secret treaties, were
answering aggression by schemes of aggression,
were seeing in the treacherous violence of Germany
only the justification for countervailing evil acts.
To them it was only another war for " ascendancy."
That was three years and a half ago, and since then
this " war of ideas " has gone on to a phase few of
us had dared hope for in those opening days. The
Russian revolution put a match to that pile of
secret treaties and indeed to all the imperialist plans
of the Allies ; in the end it will burn them all. The
greatest of the Western Allies is now the United
States of America, and the Americans have come
into this war simply for an idea. Three years and a
half ago a few of us were saying this was a war against
the idea of imperialism, not German imperialism
merely, but British and French and Russian imperialism, and we were saying this not because it
was so, but because we hoped to see it become so.
To-day we can say so, because now it is so.

In those days, moreover, we said this is the
" war to end war," and we still did not know clearly
how. We thought in terms of treaties and alliances.
It is largely the detachment and practical genius
of the great English-speaking nation across the

Atlantic that has carried the world on beyond and replaced that phrase by the phrase, "The League of Nations," a phrase suggesting plainly the organization of a sufficient instrument by which war may be ended for ever. In 1913 talk of a World League of Nations would have seemed, to the extremest pitch, "Utopian." To-day the project has an air not only of being so practicable, but of being so urgent and necessary and so manifestly the sane thing before mankind that not to be busied upon it, not to be making it more widely known and better understood, not to be working out its problems and bringing it about, is to be living outside of the contemporary life of the world. For a book upon any other subject at the present time some apology may be necessary, but a book upon this subject is as natural a thing to produce now as a pair of skates in winter when the ice begins to bear.

All we writers find ourselves engaged perforce in some part or other of a world-wide propaganda of this the most creative and hopeful of political ideas that has ever dawned upon the consciousness of mankind. With no concerted plan we feel called upon to serve it. And in no connection would one so like to think oneself un-original as in this connection. It would be a dismaying thing to realize that one were writing anything here which was not the possible thought of great multitudes

of other people, and capable of becoming the
common thought of mankind.   One writes in
such a book as this not to express oneself but
to swell a chorus.   The idea of the League of
Nations is so great a one that it may well
override the pretensions and command the alle-
giance of kings ; much more does it claim the
self-subjugation of the journalistic writer.   Our
innumerable books upon this great edifice of a
World Peace do not constitute a scramble for
attention, but an attempt to express in every
variety of phrase and aspect this one system of
ideas which now possesses us all.   In the same way
the elementary facts and ideas of the science of
chemistry might conceivably be put completely
and fully into one text-book, but, as a matter of
fact, it is far more convenient to tell that same
story over in a thousand different forms, in a text-
book for boys here, for a different sort or class of
boy there, for adult students, for reference, for
people expert in mathematics, for people unused
to the scientific method, and so on.   For the last
year the writer has been doing what he can—and
a number of other writers have been doing what
they can—to bring about a united declaration of
all the Atlantic Allies in favour of a League of
Nations, and to define the necessary nature of that
League.   He has, in the course of this work, written

a series of articles upon the League and upon *the necessary sacrifices of preconceptions* that the idea involves in the London press. He has also been trying to clear his own mind upon the real meaning of that ambiguous word " democracy," for which the League is to make the world "safe." The bulk of this book is made up of these discussions. For a very considerable number of readers, it may be well to admit here, it can have no possible interest ; they will have come at these questions themselves from different angles and they will have long since got to their own conclusions. But there may be others whose angle of approach may be similar to the writer's, who may have asked some or most of the questions he has had to ask, and who may be actively interested in the answers and the working out of the answers he has made to these questions. For them this book is printed.

H. G. WELLS.

May, 1918.

It is a dangerous thing to recommend specific books out of so large and various a literature as the " League of Nations" idea has already produced, but the reader who wishes to reach beyond the range of this book, or who does not like its tone and method, will probably find something to meet his needs and tastes better in Marburg's " League of Nations," a straightforward account of the American side of the movement by the former United States Minister in Belgium, on the one hand, or in the concluding parts of Mr. Fayle's " Great Settlement " (1915), a frankly sceptical treatment from the British Imperialist point of view, on the other. An illuminating discussion, advocating peace treaties rather than a league, is Sir Walter Phillimore's "Three Centuries of Treaties." Two excellent books from America, that chance to be on my table, are Mr. Goldsmith's "League to Enforce Peace" and "A World in Ferment" by President Nicholas Murray Butler. Mater's "Société des Nations" (Didier) is an able presentation of a French point of view. Brailsford's "A League of Nations" is already a classic of the movement in England, and a very full and thorough book; and Hobson's "Towards International Government" is a very sympathetic contribution from the English liberal left; but the reader must understand that these two writers seem disposed to welcome a peace with an unrevolutionized Germany, an idea to which, in common with most British people, I am bitterly opposed. Walsh's "World Rebuilt" is a good exhortation, and Mugge's "Parliament of Man" is fresh and sane and able. The omnivorous reader will find good sense and quaint English in Judge Mejdell's "*Jus Gentium,*" published in English by Olsen's of Christiania. There is an active League of Nations Society in Dublin, as well as the London and Washington ones, publishing pamphlets and conducting propaganda. All these books and pamphlets I have named happen to lie upon my study table as I write, but I have made no systematic effort to get together literature upon the subject, and probably there are just as many books as good of which I have never even heard. There must, I am sure, be statements of the League of Nations idea forthcoming from various religious standpoints, but I do not know any sufficiently well to recommend them. It is incredible that neither the Roman Catholic Church, the English Episcopal Church, nor any Nonconformist body has made any effort as an organization to forward this essentially religious end of peace on earth. And also there must be German writings upon this same topic. I mention these diverse sources not in order to present a bibliography, but because I should be sorry to have the reader think that this little book pretends to state *the* case rather than *a* case for the League of Nations.

CONTENTS

IN THE FOURTH YEAR

THE LEAGUE OF FREE NATIONS

I

THE WAY TO CONCRETE REALIZATION

MORE and more frequently does one hear this phrase, The League of Nations, used to express the outline idea of the new world that will come out of the war. There can be no doubt that the phrase has taken hold of the imaginations of great multitudes of people: it is one of those creative phrases that may alter the whole destiny of mankind. But as yet it is still a very vague phrase, a cloudy promise of peace. I make no apology therefore, for casting my discussion of it in the most general terms. The idea is the idea of united human effort to put an end to wars; the first practical question, that must precede all others, is how far can we hope to get to a concrete realization of that?

B

But first let me note the fourth word in the second title of this book. The common talk is of a " League of Nations " merely. I follow the man who is, more than any other man, the leader of English political thought throughout the world to-day, President Wilson, in inserting that significant adjective " Free." We western allies know to-day what is involved in making bargains with governments that do not stand for their peoples ; we have had all our Russian deal, for example, repudiated and thrust back upon our hands ; and it is clearly in his mind, as it must be in the minds of all reasonable men, that no mere " scrap of paper," with just a monarch's or a chancellor's endorsement, is a good enough earnest of fellowship in the league. It cannot be a diplomatist's league. The League of Nations, if it is to have any such effect as people seem to hope from it, must be, in the first place, " understanded of the people." It must be supported by sustained, deliberate explanation, and by teaching in school and church and press of the whole mass of all the peoples concerned. I underline the adjective " Free " here to set aside, once for all, any possible misconception that this modern idea of a League of Nations has any affinity to that Holy Alliance of the diplomatists, which set out to keep the peace of Europe so disastrously a century ago.

Later I will discuss the powers of the League. But before I come to that I would like to say a little about the more general question of its nature and authority. What sort of gathering will embody it ? The suggestions made range from a mere advisory body, rather like the Hague convention, which will merely pronounce on the rights and wrongs of any international conflict, to the idea of a sort of Super-State, a Parliament of Mankind, a "Super National" Authority, practically taking over the sovereignty of the existing states and empires of the world. Most people's ideas of the League fall between these extremes. They want the League to be something more than an ethical court, they want a League that will act, but on the other hand they shrink from any loss of "our independence." There seems to be a conflict here. There is a real need for many people to tidy up their ideas at this point. We cannot have our cake and eat it. If association is worth while, there must be some sacrifice of freedom to association. As a very distinguished colonial representative said to me the other day : "Here we are talking of the freedom of small nations and the 'self-determination' of peoples, and at the same time of the Council of the League of Nations and all sorts of international controls. Which do we want ? "

The answer, I think, is " Both." It is a matter of more or less, of getting the best thing at the cost of the second-best. We may want to relax an old association in order to make a newer and wider one. It is quite understandable that peoples aware of a distinctive national character and involved in some big existing political complex, should wish to disentangle themselves from one group of associations in order to enter more effectively into another, a greater, and more satisfactory one. The Finn or the Pole, who has hitherto been a rather reluctant member of the synthesis of the Russian empire, may well wish to end that attachment in order to become a free member of a world-wide brotherhood. The desire for free arrangement is not a desire for chaos. There is such a thing as untying your parcels in order to pack them better, and I do not see myself how we can possibly contemplate a great league of freedom and reason in the world without a considerable amount of such preliminary dissolution.

It happens, very fortunately for the world, that a century and a quarter ago thirteen various and very jealous states worked out the problem of a Union, and became—after an enormous, exhausting wrangle—the United States of America. Now the way they solved their riddle was by delegating and giving over jealously specified sovereign powers and

doing all that was possible to retain the residuum.
They remained essentially sovereign states. New
York, Virginia, Massachusetts, for example, remained legally independent. The practical fusion
of these peoples into one people outran the legal
bargain. It was only after long years of discussion
that the point was conceded; it was indeed only
after the Civil War that the implications were fully
established, that there resided a sovereignty in the
American people as a whole, as distinguished from
the peoples of the several states. This is a precedent that every one who talks about the League of
Nations should bear in mind. These states set
up a congress and president in Washington with
strictly delegated powers. That congress and
president they delegated to look after certain
common interests, to deal with interstate trade, to
deal with foreign powers, to maintain a supreme
court of law. Everything else—education, militia,
powers of life and death—the states retained for
themselves. To this day, for instance, the federal
courts and the federal officials have no power to
interfere to protect the lives or property of aliens
in any part of the union outside the district of
Columbia. The state governments still see to that.
The federal government has the legal right perhaps
to intervene, but it is still chary of such intervention. And these states of the American Union

were at the outset so independent-spirited that they would not even adopt a common name. To this day they have no common name. We have to call them Americans, which is a ridiculous name when we consider that Canada, Mexico, Peru, Brazil are all of them also in America. Or else we have to call them Virginians, Californians, New Englanders, and so forth. Their legal and nominal separateness weighs nothing against the real fusion that their great league has now made possible.

Now, that clearly is a precedent of the utmost value in our schemes for this council of the League of Nations. We must begin by delegating, as the States began by delegating. It is a far cry to the time when we shall talk and think of the Sovereign People of the Earth. That council of the League of Nations will be a tie as strong, we hope, but certainly not so close and multiplex as the early tie of the States at Washington. It will begin by having certain delegated powers and no others. It will be an "*ad hoc*" body. Later its powers may grow as mankind becomes accustomed to it. But at first it will have, directly or mediately, all the powers that seem necessary to restrain the world from war—and unless I know nothing of patriotic jealousies it will have not a scrap of power more. The danger is much more that its powers will be insufficient than that they will be excessive. Of that later. What I want to discuss here now is the constitution of this delegated body. I want to discuss that first in order to set aside out of the discussion certain fantastic notions that will otherwise get very seriously in our way. Fantastic as they are, they have played a large part in reducing the Hague Tribunal to an ineffective squeak amidst the thunders of this war.

A number of gentlemen scheming out world unity in studies have begun their proposals with the simple suggestion that each sovereign power should send one member to the projected parliament of mankind. This has a pleasant democratic air; one sovereign state, one vote. Now let us run over a list of sovereign states and see to what this leads us. We find our list includes the British Empire, with a population of four hundred millions, of which probably half can read and write some language or other; Bogota with a population of a million, mostly poets; Hayti with a population of a million and a third, almost entirely illiterate and liable at any time to further political disruption; Andorra with a population of four or five thousand souls. The mere suggestion of equal representation between such " powers " is enough to make the British Empire burst into a thousand (voting) fragments. A certain concession to population, one must admit, was made by the theorists; a state of over three millions got, if I remember rightly, two delegates, and if over twenty, three, and some of the small states were given a kind of intermittent appearance, they only came every other time or something of that sort; but at The Hague things still remained in such a posture that three or four minute and backward states could outvote the British Empire or the United States. Therein lies the clue to the insignificance of The Hague. Such projects as these are idle projects and we must put them out of our heads; they are against nature; the great nations will not suffer them for a moment.

But when we dismiss this idea of representation by states, we are left with the problem of the proportion of representation and of relative weight in the Council of the League on our hands. It is the sort of problem that appeals terribly to the ingenious. We cannot solve it by making population a basis, because that will give a monstrous importance to the illiterate millions of India and China. Ingenious statistical schemes have been framed in which the number of university graduates and the steel output come in as multipliers, but for my own part I am not greatly impressed by statistical schemes. At the risk of seeming something

of a Prussian, I would like to insist upon certain
brute facts.   The business of the League of Nations
is to keep the peace of the world and nothing else.
No power will ever dare to break the peace of the
world if the powers that are capable of making war
under modern conditions say " *No.*"   And there
are only four powers certainly capable at the present
time of producing the men and materials needed
for a modern war in sufficient abundance to go on
fighting : Britain, France, Germany, and the United
States.   There are three others which are very
doubtfully capable : Italy, Japan, and Austria.
Russia I will mark—it is all that one can do with
Russia just now—with a note of interrogation.
Some day China may be war capable—I hope
never, but it is a possibility.   Personally I don't
think that any other power on earth would have a
ghost of a chance to resist the will—if it could be
an honestly united will—of the first-named four.
All the rest fight by the sanction of and by association with these leaders.   They can only fight
because of the split will of the war-complete powers.
Some are forced to fight by that very division.

No one can vie with me in my appreciation of
the civilization of Switzerland, Sweden, or Holland,
but the plain fact of the case is that such powers
are absolutely incapable of uttering an effective
protest against war.   Far less so are your Haytis

and Liberias. The preservation of the world-peace rests with the great powers and with the great powers alone. If they have the will for peace, it is peace. If they have not, it is conflict. The four powers I have named can now, if they see fit, dictate the peace of the world for ever.

Let us keep our grip on that. Peace is the business of the great powers primarily. Steel output, university graduates, and so forth may be convenient secondary criteria, may be useful ways of measuring war efficiency, but the meat and substance of the Council of the League of Nations must embody the wills of those leading peoples. They can give an enduring peace to the little nations and the whole of mankind. It can arrive in no other way. So I take it that the Council of an ideal League of Nations must consist chiefly of the representatives of the great belligerent powers, and that the representatives of the minor allies and of the neutrals—essential though their presence will be—must not be allowed to swamp the voices of these larger masses of mankind.

And this state of affairs may come about more easily than logical, statistical-minded people may be disposed to think. Our first impulse, when we discuss the League of Nations idea, is to think of some very elaborate and definite scheme of members on the model of existing legislative bodies, called together one hardly knows how, and sitting in a specially built League of Nations Congress House. All schemes are more methodical than reality. We think of somebody, learned and " expert," in spectacles, with a thin clear voice, reading over the " Projected Constitution of a League of Nations ": to an attentive and respectful Peace Congress. But there is a more natural way to a league than that. Instead of being made like a machine, the League of Nations may come about like a marriage. The Peace Congress that must sooner or later meet may itself become, after a time, the Council of a League of Nations. The League of Nations may come upon us by degrees, almost imperceptibly. I am strongly obsessed by the idea that that Peace Congress will necessarily become—and that it is highly desirable that it should become—a most prolonged and persistent gathering. Why should it not become at length a permanent gathering, inviting representatives to aid its deliberations from the neutral states, and gradually adjusting itself to conditions of permanency ?

I can conceive no such Peace Congress as those that have settled up after other wars, settling up after this war. Not only has the war been enormously bigger than any other war, but it has struck deeper at the foundations of social and economic life. I doubt if we begin to realize how much of the old system is dead to-day, how much has to be remade. Since the beginnings of history there has been a credible promise of gold payments underneath our financial arrangements. It is now an incredible promise. The value of a pound note waves about while you look at it. What will happen to it when peace comes no man can tell. Nor what will happen to the mark. The rouble has gone into the Abyss. Our giddy money specialists clutch their handfuls of paper and watch it flying down the steep. Much as we may hate the Germans, some of us will have to sit down with some of the enemy to arrange a common scheme for the preservation of credit in money. And I presume that it is not proposed to end this war in a wild scramble of buyers for such food as remains in the world. There is a shortage now, a greater shortage ahead of the world, and there will be shortages of supply at the source and transport in food and all raw materials for some years to come. The Peace Congress will have to sit and organize a share-out and distribution and reorganization of these shattered supplies. It will have to Rhondda the nations. Probably, too, we shall have to deal collectively with a pestilence before we are out of the mess. Then there are such little jobs as the reconstruction of Belgium and Serbia. There are considerable rectifications of boundaries to be made. There are fresh states to be created, in Poland and Armenia for example. About all these smaller states, new and old, that the peace must call into being, there must be a system of guarantees of the most difficult and complicated sort.

I do not see the Press Congress getting through such matters as these in a session of weeks or months. The idea the Germans betrayed at Brest, that things were going to be done in the Versailles fashion by great moustached heroes frowning and drawing lines with a large black soldierly thumbnail across maps, is—old-fashioned. They have made their eastern treaties, it is true, in this mode, but they are still looking for some really responsible government to keep them now that they are made. From first to last clearly the main peace negotiations are going to follow unprecedented courses. This preliminary discussion of war aims by means of great public speeches, that has been getting more and more explicit now for many months, is quite unprecedented. Apparently all the broad preliminaries are to be stated and accepted in the sight of all mankind before even an armistice occurs on the main, the western front. The German diplomatists hate this process. So do a lot of ours. So do some of the diplomatic Frenchmen. The German junkers are dodging and lying, they

are fighting desperately to keep back everything
they possibly can for the bargaining and bullying
and table-banging of the council chamber, but
that way there is no peace.   And when at last
Germany says snip sufficiently to the Allies' snap,
and the Peace Congress begins, it will almost certainly be as unprecedented as its prelude.   Before
it meets, the broad lines of the settlement will
have been drawn plainly with the approval of the
mass of mankind.

II

THE LEAGUE MUST BE REPRESENTATIVE

A PEACE Congress, growing permanent, then, may prove to be the most practical and convenient embodiment of this idea of a League of Nations that has taken possession of the imagination of the world. A most necessary preliminary to a Peace Congress, with such possibilities inherent in it, must obviously be the meeting and organization of a preliminary League of the Allied Nations. That point I would now enlarge.

Half a world peace is better than none. There seems no reason whatever why the world should wait for the Central Powers before it begins this necessary work. Mr. McCurdy has been asking lately, " Why not the League of Nations *now* ? " That is a question a great number of people would like to echo very heartily. The nearer the Allies can come to a League of Free Nations before the Peace Congress the more prospect there is that that body will approximate in nature to a League of Nations for the whole world.

In one most unexpected quarter the same idea has been endorsed. The King's Speech on the prorogation of Parliament this February was one of the most remarkable royal utterances that have ever been made from the British throne. There was less of the old-fashioned King and more of the modern President about it than the most republican-minded of us could have anticipated. For the first time in a King's Speech we heard of the " democracies " of the world, and there was a clear claim that the Allies at present fighting the Central Powers did themselves constitute a League of Nations.

But we must admit that at present they do so only in a very rhetorical sense. There is no real council of empowered representatives, and nothing in the nature of a united front has been prepared. Unless we provide beforehand for something more effective, Italy, France, the United States, Japan, and this country will send separate groups of representatives, with separate instructions, unequal status, and very probably conflicting views upon many subjects, to the ultimate peace discussions. It is quite conceivable—it is a very serious danger—that at this discussion skilful diplomacy on the part of the Central Powers may open a cleft among the Allies that has never appeared during the actual war. Have the British settled, for example, with Italy and France for the supply of metallurgical coal after the war ? Those countries must have it somehow. Across the board Germany can make some tempting bids in that respect. Or take another question : Have the British arrived at common views with France, Belgium, Portugal, and South Africa about the administration of Central Africa ? Suppose Germany makes sudden proposals affecting native labour that win over the Portuguese and the Boers ? There are a score of such points upon which we shall find the Allied representatives haggling with each other in the presence of the enemy if they have not been settled beforehand.

It is the plainest common sense that we should be fixing up all such matters with our Allies now, and knitting together a common front for the final deal with German Imperialism. And these things are not to be done effectively and bindingly nowadays by official gentlemen in discreet undertones. They need to be done with the full knowledge and authority of the participating peoples.

The Russian example has taught the world the instability of diplomatic bargains in a time of such fundamental issues as the present. There is little hope and little strength in hole-and-corner bargainings between the officials or politicians who happen to be at the head of this or that nation for the time

c

being.   Our Labour people will not stand this sort
of thing and they will not be bound by it.   There
will be the plain danger of repudiation for all
arrangements made in that fashion.   A gathering
of somebody or other approved by the British
Foreign Office and of somebody or other approved
by the French Foreign Office, of somebody with
vague powers from America, and so on and so on,
will be an entirely ineffective gathering.   But that
is the sort of gathering of the Allies we have been
having hitherto, and that is the sort of gathering
that is likely to continue unless there is a considerable expression of opinion in favour of something more representative and responsible.

Even our Foreign Office must be aware that
in every country in the world there is now bitter
suspicion of and keen hostility towards merely
diplomatic representatives.   One of the most significant features of the time is the evident desire
of the Labour movement in every European country
to take part in a collateral conference of Labour
that shall meet when and where the Peace Congress
does and deliberate and comment on its proceedings.   For a year now the demand of the masses
for such a Labour conference has been growing.
It marks a distrust of officialdom whose intensity
officialdom would do well to ponder.   But it is the
natural consequence of, it is the popular attempt

at a corrective to, the aloofness and obscurity that have hitherto been so evil a characteristic of international negotiations. I do not think Labour and intelligent people anywhere are going to be fobbed off with an old-fashioned diplomatic gathering as being that League of Free Nations they demand.

On the other hand, I do not contemplate this bi-cameral conference with the diplomatists trying to best and humbug the Labour people as well as each other and the Labour people getting more and more irritated, suspicious, and extremist, with anything but dread. The Allied countries must go into the conference *solid*, and they can only hope to do that by heeding and incorporating Labour ideas before they come to the conference. The only alternative that I can see to this unsatisfactory prospect of a Peace Congress sitting side by side with a dissentient and probably revolutionary Labour and Socialist convention—both gatherings with unsatisfactory credentials contradicting one another and drifting to opposite extremes—is that the delegates the Allied Powers send to the Peace Conference (the same delegates which, if they are wise, they will have previously sent to a preliminary League of Allied Nations to discuss their common action at the Peace Congress), should be elected *ad hoc* upon democratic lines.

I know that this will be a very shocking proposal to all our able specialists in foreign policy. They will talk at once about the " ignorance " of people like the Labour leaders and myself about such matters, and so on. What do we know of the treaty of so-and-so that was signed in the year seventeen something ?—and so on. To which the answer is that we ought not to have been kept ignorant of these things. A day will come when the Foreign Offices of all countries will have to recognize that what the people do not know of international agreements " ain't facts." A secret treaty is only binding upon the persons in the secret. But what I, as a sample common person, am not ignorant of is this : that the business that goes on at the Peace Congress will either make or mar the lives of everyone I care for in the world, and that somehow, by representative or what not, *I have to be there*. The Peace Congress deals with the blood and happiness of my children and the future of my world. Speaking as one of the hundreds of millions of " rank outsiders " in public affairs, I do not mean to respect any peace treaty that may end this war unless I am honestly represented at its making. I think everywhere there is a tendency in people to follow the Russian example to this extent and to repudiate bargains in which they have had no voice.

I do not see that any genuine realization of the hopes with which all this talk about the League of Nations is charged can be possible, unless the two bodies which should naturally lead up to the League of Nations—that is to say, firstly, the Conference of the Allies, and then the Peace Congress—are elected bodies, speaking confidently for the whole mass of the peoples behind them. It may be a troublesome thing to elect them, but it will involve much more troublesome consequences if they are not elected. This, I think, is one of the considerations for which many people's minds are still unprepared. But unless we are to have over again after all this bloodshed and effort some such " Peace with Honour " foolery as we had performed by " Dizzy " and Salisbury at that fatal Berlin Conference in which this present war was begotten, we must sit up to this novel proposal of electoral representation in the peace negotiations. Something more than common sense binds our statesmen to this idea. They are morally pledged to it. President Wilson and our British and French spokesmen alike have said over and over again that they want to deal not with the Hohenzollerns but with the German people. In other words, we have demanded elected representatives from the German people with whom we may deal, and how can we make a demand of that sort unless we on our part are already prepared to send our own elected representatives to meet them ? It is up to us to indicate by our own practice how we on our side, professing as we do to act for democracies, to make democracy safe on the earth, and so on, intend to meet this new occasion.

Yet it has to be remarked that, so far, not one of the League of Nations projects I have seen have included any practicable proposals for the appointment of delegates either to that ultimate body or to its two necessary predecessors, the Council of the Allies and the Peace Congress. It is evident that here, again, we are neglecting to get on with something of very urgent importance. I will venture, therefore, to say a word or two here about the possible way in which a modern community may appoint its international representatives.

And here, again, I turn from any European precedents to that political outcome of the British mind, the Constitution of the United States. (Because we must always remember that while our political institutions in Britain are a patch-up of feudalism, Tudor, Stuart, and Hanoverian monarchist traditions and urgent merely European necessities, a patch-up that has been made quasi-democratic in a series of after-thoughts, the

American Constitution is a real, deliberate creation of the English-speaking intelligence.) The President of the United States, then, we have to note, is elected in a most extraordinary way, and in a way that has now the justification of very great successes indeed. On several occasions the United States has achieved indisputable greatness in its Presidents, and very rarely has it failed to set up very leaderly and distinguished men. It is worth while, therefore, to inquire how this President is elected. He is neither elected directly by the people nor appointed by any legislative body. He is chosen by a special college elected by the people. This college exists to elect him; it meets, elects him, and disperses. (I will not here go into the preliminary complications that makes the election of a President follow upon a preliminary election of two Presidential Candidates. The point I am making here is that he is a specially selected man chosen *ad hoc.*) Is there any reason why we should not adopt this method in this new necessity we are under of sending representatives, first, to the long overdue and necessary Allied Council, then to the Peace Congress, and then to the hoped-for Council of the League of Nations ?

I am anxious here only to start for discussion the idea of an electoral representation of the nations upon these three bodies that must in succession set themselves to define, organize, and maintain the peace of the world. I do not wish to complicate the question by any too explicit advocacy of methods of election or the like. In the United States this college which elects the President is elected on the same register of voters as that which elects the Senate and Congress, and at the same time. But I suppose if we are to give a popular mandate to the three or five or twelve or twenty (or whatever number it is) men to whom we are going to entrust our Empire's share in this great task of the peace negotiations, it will be more decisive of the will of the whole nation if the college that had to appoint them is elected at a special election. I suppose that the great British commonweals over-seas, at present not represented in Parliament, would also and separately at the same time elect colleges to appoint their representatives. I suppose there would be at least one Indian representative elected, perhaps by some special electoral conference of Indian princes and leading men. The chief defect of the American Presidential election is that as the old single vote method of election is employed it has to be fought on purely party lines. He is the select man of the Democratic half, or of the Republican half of the nation. He is not the select man of the whole nation. It would give a far more representative character to the electoral college if it could be elected by fair modern methods, if for this particular purpose parliamentary constituencies could be grouped and the clean scientific method of proportional representation could be used. But I suppose the party politician in this, as in most of our affairs, must still have his pound of our flesh—and we must reckon with him later for the bloodshed.

These are all, however, secondary considerations. The above paragraph is, so to speak, in the nature of a footnote. The fundamental matter, if we are to get towards any realization of this ideal of a world peace sustained by a League of Nations, is to get straight away to the conception of direct special electoral mandates in this matter. At present all the political luncheon and dinner parties in London are busy with smirking discussions of "Who is to go?" The titled ladies are particularly busy. They are talking about it as if we poor, ignorant, tax-paying, blood-paying common people did not exist. "L. G.," they say, will of course "*insist* on going," but there is much talk of the "Old Man." People are getting quite nice again about "the Old Man's feelings." It would be such a pretty thing to send him. But if "L. G." goes we want him to go with something more than a backing of intrigues and snatched authority. And I do not think the mass of people have any

enthusiasm for the Old Man.   It is difficult again—
by the dinner-party standards—to know how Lord
Curzon can be restrained.   But we common people
do not care if he is restrained to the point of
extinction.   Probably there will be nobody who
talks or understands Russian among the British
representatives.   But, of course, the British
governing class has washed its hands of the
Russians.   They were always very difficult, and
now they are "impossible, my dear, perfectly
impossible."

No !   That sort of thing will not do now.
This Peace Congress is too big a job for party
politicians and society and county families.   The
bulk of British opinion cannot go on being represented for ever by President Wilson.   We cannot
always look to the Americans to express our ideas
and do our work for democracy.   The foolery of
the Berlin Treaty must not be repeated.   We
cannot have another popular Prime Minister come
triumphing back to England with a gross of pink
spectacles—through which we may survey the
prospect of the next great war.   The League of
Free Nations means something very big and solid ;
it is not a rhetorical phrase to be used to pacify a
restless, distressed, and anxious public, and to be
sneered out of existence when that use is past.
When the popular mind now demands a League

of Free Nations it demands a reality. The only
way to that reality is through the direct participa-
tion of the nation as a whole in the settlement, and
that is possible only through the direct election for
this particular issue of representative and responsible men.

III

THE NECESSARY POWERS OF THE LEAGUE

If this phrase, "the League of Free Nations," is to signify anything more than a rhetorical flourish, then certain consequences follow that have to be faced now. No man can join a partnership and remain an absolutely free man. You cannot bind yourself to do this and not to do that and to consult and act with your associates in certain eventualities without a loss of your sovereign freedom. People in this country and in France do not seem to be sitting up manfully to these necessary propositions.

If this League of Free Nations is really to be an effectual thing for the preservation of the peace of the world it must possess power and exercise power, powers must be delegated to it. Otherwise it will only help, with all other half-hearted good resolutions, to pave the road of mankind to hell. Nothing in all the world so strengthens evil as the half-hearted attempts of good to make good.

It scarcely needs repeating here—it has been

28

so generally said—that no League of Free Nations can hope to keep the peace unless every member of it is indeed a free member, represented by duly elected persons. Nobody, of course, asks to "dictate the internal government" of any country to that country. If Germans, for instance, like to wallow in absolutism after the war they can do so. But if they or any other peoples wish to take part in a permanent League of Free Nations it is only reasonable to insist that so far as their representatives on the council go they must be duly elected under conditions that are by the standards of the general league satisfactorily democratic. That seems to be only the common sense of the matter. Every court is a potential conspiracy against freedom, and the League cannot tolerate merely court appointments. If courts are to exist anywhere in the new world of the future, they will be wise to stand aloof from international meddling. Of course if a people, after due provision for electoral representation, choose to elect dynastic candidates, that is an altogether different matter.

And now let us consider what are the powers that must be delegated to this proposed council of a League of Free Nations, if that is really effectually to prevent war and to organize and establish and make peace permanent in the world.

Firstly, then, it must be able to adjudicate upon

all international disputes whatever. Its first function must clearly be that. Before a war can break out there must be the possibility of a world decision upon its rights and wrongs. The League, therefore, will have as its primary function to maintain a Supreme Court, whose decisions will be final, before which every sovereign power may appear as plaintiff against any other sovereign power or group of powers. The plea, I take it, will always be in the form that the defendant power or powers is engaged in proceedings " calculated to lead to a breach of the peace," and calling upon the League for an injunction against such proceedings. I suppose the proceedings that can be brought into court in this way fall under such headings as these that follow ; restraint of trade by injurious tariffs or suchlike differentiations or by interference with through traffic, improper treatment of the subjects *or their property* (here I put a query) of the plaintiff nation in the defendant state, aggressive military or naval preparation, disorder spreading over the frontier, trespass (as, for instance, by airships), propaganda of disorder, espionage, permitting the organization of injurious activities, such as raids or piracy. Clearly all such actions must come within the purview of any world-supreme court organized to prevent war. But in addition there is a more doubtful and delicate class of case, arising out of the discontent of patches of one race or religion in the dominions of another. How far may the supreme court of the world attend to grievances between subject and sovereign ?

Such cases are highly probable, and no large, vague propositions about the " self-determination " of peoples can meet all the cases. In Macedonia, for instance, there is a jumble of Albanian, Serbian, Bulgarian, Greek and Rumanian villages always jostling one another and maintaining an intense irritation between the kindred nations close at hand. And quite a large number of areas and cities in the world, it has to be remembered, are not homogeneous at all. Will the great nations of the world have the self-abnegation to permit a scattered subject population to appeal against the treatment of its ruling power to the Supreme Court ? This is a much more serious interference with sovereignty than intervention in an external quarrel. Could a Greek village in Bulgarian Macedonia plead in the Supreme Court ? Could the Armenians in Constantinople, or the Jews in Roumania, or the Poles in West Prussia, or the negroes in Georgia, or the Indians in the Transvaal make such an appeal ? Could any Indian population in India appeal ? Personally I should like to see the power of the Supreme Court extend as far as this. I do not see how we can possibly prevent a kindred nation pleading for the scattered people of its own race and culture, or any nation presenting a case on behalf of some otherwise unrepresented people—the United States, for example, presenting a case on behalf of the Armenians. But I doubt if many people have made up their minds yet to see the powers of the Supreme Court of the League of Nations go so far as this. I doubt if, to begin with, it will be possible to provide for these cases. I would like to see it done, but I doubt if the majority of the sovereign peoples concerned will reconcile their national pride with the idea, at least so far as their own subject populations go.

Here, you see, I do no more than ask a question. It is a difficult one, and it has to be answered before we can clear the way to the League of Free Nations.

But the Supreme Court, whether it is to have the wider or the narrower scope here suggested, would be merely the central function of the League of Free Nations. Behind the decisions of the Supreme Court must lie power. And here come fresh difficulties for patriotic digestions. The armies and navies of the world must be at the disposal of the League of Free Nations, and that opens up a new large area of delegated authority. The first impulse of any power disposed to challenge the decisions of the Supreme Court will be, of course, to arm; and it is difficult to imagine how the League of Free Nations can exercise any practical authority unless it has power to restrain such armament. The League of Free Nations must, in fact, if it is to be a working reality, have power to define and limit the military and naval and aerial equipment of every country in the world. This means something more than a restriction of state forces. It must have power and freedom to investigate the military and naval and aerial establishments of all its constituent powers. It must also have effective control over every armament industry. And armament industries are not always easy to define. Are aeroplanes, for example, armament? Its powers, I suggest, must extend even to a restraint upon the belligerent propaganda which is the natural advertisement campaign of every armament industry. It must have the right, for example, to raise the question of the proprietorship of newspapers by armament interests. Disarmament is, in fact, a necessary factor of any League of Free Nations, and you cannot have disarmament unless you are prepared to see the powers of the council of the League extend thus far. The very existence of the League presupposes that it and it alone is to have and to exercise military force. Any other belligerency or preparation or incitement to belligerency becomes rebellion, and any other arming a threat of rebellion, in a world League of Free Nations.

D

But here, again, has the general mind yet thought
out all that is involved in this proposition ?   In all
the great belligerent countries the armament industries are now huge interests with enormous
powers.   Krupp's business alone is as powerful a
thing in Germany as the Crown.   In every country
a heavily subsidized " patriotic " press will fight
desperately against giving powers so extensive and
thorough as those here suggested to an international
body.   So long, of course, as the League of Free
Nations remains a project in the air, without body
or parts, such a press will sneer at it gently as
" Utopian," and even patronize it kindly.   But
so soon as the League takes on the shape its
general proposition makes logically necessary, the
armament interest will take fright.   Then it is we
shall hear the drum patriotic loud in defence of the
human blood trade.   Are we to hand over these
most intimate affairs of ours to " a lot of foreigners " ?   Among these " foreigners " who will be
appealed to to terrify the patriotic souls of the
British will be the " Americans."   Are we men
of English blood and tradition to see our affairs
controlled by such " foreigners " as Wilson,
Lincoln, Webster and Washington ?   Perish the
thought !   When they might be controlled by
Disraelis, Wettins, Mount-Battens, and what not !
And so on and so on.   Krupp's agents and the

agents of the kindred firms in Great Britain and France will also be very busy with the national pride of France. In Germany they have already created a colossal suspicion of England.

Here is a giant in the path. . . .

But let us remember that it is only necessary to defeat the propaganda of this vile and dangerous industry in four great countries. And for the common citizen, touched on the tenderest part of his patriotic susceptibilities, there are certain irrefutable arguments. Whether the ways of the world in the years to come are to be the paths of peace or the paths of war is not going to alter this essential fact, that the great educated world communities, with a social and industrial organization on a war-capable scale, are going to dominate human affairs. Whether they spend their power in killing or in educating and creating, France, Germany, however much we may resent it, the two great English-speaking communities, Italy, Japan China, and presently perhaps a renascent Russia, are jointly going to control the destinies of mankind. Whether that joint control comes through arms or through the law is a secondary consideration. To refuse to bring our affairs into a common council does not make us independent of foreigners. It makes us more dependent upon them, as a very little consideration will show.

I am suggesting here that the League of Free Nations shall practically control the army, navy, air forces, and armament industry of every nation in the world. What is the alternative to that? To do as we please? No, the alternative is that any malignant country will be free to force upon all the rest just the maximum amount of armament it chooses to adopt. Since 1871 France, we say, has been free in military matters. What has been the value of that freedom? The truth is, she has been the bond-slave of Germany, bound to watch Germany as a slave watches a master, bound to launch submarine for submarine and cast gun for gun, to sweep all her youth into her army, to subdue her trade, her literature, her education, her whole life to the necessity of preparations imposed upon her by her drill-master over the Rhine. And Michael, too, has been a slave to his imperial master for the self-same reason, for the reason that Germany and France were both so proudly sovereign and independent. Both countries have been slaves to Kruppism and Zabernism—*because they were sovereign and free!* So it will always be. So long as patriotic cant can keep the common man jealous of international controls over his belligerent possibilities, so long will he be the helpless slave of the foreign threat, and "Peace" remain a mere name for the resting phase between wars.

But power over the military resources of the
world is by no means the limit of the necessary
powers of an effective League of Free Nations.
There are still more indigestible implications in
the idea, and, since they have got to be digested
sooner or later if civilization is not to collapse,
there is no reason why we should not begin to bite
upon them now. I was much interested to read
the British press upon the alleged proposal of
the German Chancellor that we should give
up (presumably to Germany) Gibraltar, Malta,
Egypt, and suchlike key possessions. It seemed to
excite several of our politicians extremely. I read
over the German Chancellor's speech very care-
fully, so far as it was available, and it is clear
that he did not propose anything of the sort.
Wilfully or blindly our press and our demagogues
screamed over a false issue. The Chancellor was
defending the idea of the Germans remaining in
Belgium and Lorraine because of the strategic and
economic importance of those regions to Germany,
and he was arguing that before we English got
into such a feverish state of indignation about that,
we should first ask ourselves what we were doing
in Gibraltar, etc., etc. That is a different thing
altogether. And it is an argument that is not to
be disposed of by misrepresentation. The British
have to think hard over this quite legitimate

German *tu quoque*.   It is no good getting into a patriotic bad temper and refusing to answer that question.   We British people are so persuaded of the purity and unselfishness with which we discharge our imperial responsibilities, we have been so trained in imperial self-satisfaction, we know so certainly that all our subject nations call us blessed, that it is a little difficult for us to see just how the fact that we are, for example, so deeply rooted in Egypt looks to an outside intelligence.   Of course the German imperialist idea is a wicked and aggressive idea, as Lord Robert Cecil has explained; they want to set up all over the earth coaling stations and strategic points, *on the pattern of ours.* Well, they argue, we are only trying to do what you British have done.   If we are not to do so— because it is aggression and so on and so on—is not the time ripe for you to make some concessions to the public opinion of the world?   That is the German argument.   Either, they say, tolerate this idea of a Germany with advantageous posts and possessions round and about the earth, or reconsider your own position.

Well, at the risk of rousing much patriotic wrath, I must admit that I think we *have* to reconsider our position.   Our argument is that in India, Egypt, Africa and elsewhere, we stand for order and civilization, we are the trustees of freedom, the agents of knowledge and efficiency. On the whole the record of British rule is a pretty respectable one ; I am not ashamed of our record. Nevertheless *the case is altering*.

It is quite justifiable for us British, no doubt, if we do really play the part of honest trustees, to remain in Egypt and in India under existing conditions ; it is even possible for us to glance at the helplessness of Arabia, Palestine, and Mesopotamia, as yet incapable of self-government, helpless as new-born infants. But our case, our only justifiable case, is that we are trustees because there is no better trustee possible. And the creation of a council of a League of Free Nations would be like the creation of a Public Trustee for the world. The creation of a League of Free Nations must necessarily be the creation of an authority that may legitimately call existing empires to give an account of their stewardship. For an unchecked fragmentary control of tropical and chaotic regions, it substitutes the possibility of a general authority. And this must necessarily alter the problems not only of the politically immature nations and the control of the tropics, but also of the regulation of the sea ways, the regulation of the coming air routes, and the distribution of staple products in the world. I will not go in detail over the items of this list, because the reader can fill in the essentials of the argument from what has gone before. I want simply to suggest how widely this project of a League of Free Nations swings when once you have let it swing freely in your mind ! And if you do not let it swing freely in your mind, it remains nothing—a sentimental gesture.

The plain truth is that the League of Free Nations, if it is to be a reality, if it is to effect a real pacification of the world, must do no less than supersede Empire ; it must end not only this new German imperialism, which is struggling so savagely and powerfully to possess the earth, but it must also wind up British imperialism and French imperialism, which do now so largely and inaggressively possess it. And, moreover, this idea queries the adjective of Belgian, Portuguese, French, and British Central Africa alike, just as emphatically as it queries " German." Still more effectually does the League forbid those creations of the futurist imagination, the imperialism of Italy and Greece, which make such threatening gestures at the world of our children. Are these incompatibilities understood ? Until people have faced the clear antagonism that exists between imperialism and internationalism, they have not begun to suspect the real significance of this project of the League of Free Nations. They have not begun to realize that peace also has its price.

IV

THE LABOUR VIEW OF MIDDLE AFRICA

I WAS recently privileged to hear the views of one of those titled and influential ladies—with a general education at about the fifth standard level, plus a little French, German, Italian, and music—who do so much to make our England what it is at the present time, upon the Labour idea of an international control of " tropical " Africa. She was loud and derisive about the " ignorance " of Labour. " What can *they* know about foreign politics ? " she said, with gestures to indicate her conception of *them*.

I was moved to ask her what she would do about Africa. " Leave it to Lord Robert ! " she said, leaning forward impressively. " *Leave it to the people who know.*"

Unhappily I share the evident opinion of Labour that we are not blessed with any profoundly wise class of people who have definite knowledge and clear intentions about Africa, that these " *people who know* " are mostly a pretentious bluff, and so, in spite of a very earnest desire to take refuge in my " ignorance " from the burthen of thinking about African problems, I find myself obliged, like most other people, to do so. In the interests of our country, our children, and the world, we common persons *have* to have opinions about these matters. A muddle-up in Africa this year may kill your son and mine in the course of the next decade. I know this is not a claim to be interested in things African, such as the promoter of a tropical railway or an oil speculator has ; still it is a claim. And for the life of me I cannot see what is wrong about the Labour proposals, or what alternative exists that can give even a hope of peace in and about Africa.

The gist of the Labour proposal is an international control of Africa between the Zambesi and the Sahara. This has been received with loud protests by men whose work one is obliged to respect, by Sir Harry Johnston, for example, and Sir Alfred Sharpe, and with something approaching a shriek of hostility by Mr. Cunninghame Graham. But I think these gentlemen have not perhaps given the Labour proposal quite as much attention as they have spent upon the details of African conditions. I think they have jumped to conclusions at the mere sound of the word " international." There have been some gross failures in the past to set up international administrations in Africa and the Near East. And these gentlemen think at once of some new Congo administration and of nondescript police forces commanded by cosmopolitan adventurers. (See Joseph Conrad's " Outpost of Civilization.") They think of internationalism with greedy Great Powers in the background outside the internationalized area, intriguing to create disorder and mischief with ideas of an ultimate annexation. But I doubt if such nightmares do any sort of justice to the Labour intention.

And the essential thing I would like to point out to these authorities upon African questions is that not one of them even hints at any other formula which covers the broad essentials of the African riddle.

What are these broad essentials ? What are the ends that *must* be achieved if Africa is not to continue a festering sore in the body of mankind ?

The first most obvious danger of Africa is the militarization of the black. General Smuts has pointed this out plainly. The negro makes a good soldier ; he is hardy, he stands the sea, and he stands cold. (There was a negro in the little party which reached the North Pole.) It is absolutely essential to the peace of the world that there should be no arming of the negroes beyond the minimum necessary for the policing of Africa. But how is this to be watched and prevented if there is no overriding body representing civilization to say "Stop" to the beginnings of any such militarization? I do not see how Sir Harry Johnston, Sir Alfred Sharpe, and the other authorities can object to at least an international African "Disarmament Commission" to watch, warn, and protest. At least they must concede that.

But in practice this involves something else. A practical consequence of this disarmament idea must be an effective control of the importation of arms into the "tutelage" areas of Africa. That rat at the dykes of civilization, that ultimate expression of political scoundrelism, the Gun-Runner, has to be kept under and stamped out in Africa as everywhere. A Disarmament Commission that has no forces available to prevent the arms trade will be just another Hague Convention, just another vague, well-intentioned, futile gesture.

And closely connected with this function of controlling the arms trade is another great necessity of Africa under "tutelage," and that is the necessity of a common collective agreement not to demoralize the native population. That demoralization, physical and moral, has already gone far. The whole negro population of Africa is now rotten with diseases introduced by Arabs and Europeans during the last century, and such African statesmen

as Sir Harry Johnston are eloquent upon the necessity of saving the blacks—and the baser whites—
from the effects of trade gin and similar alluring
articles of commerce.   Moreover, from Africa there
is always something new in the way of tropical
diseases, and presently Africa, if we let it continue
to fester as it festers now, may produce an epi-
demic that will stand exportation to a temperate
climate.   A bacterium that may kill you or me in
some novel and disgusting way may even now be
developing in some Congo muck-heap.   So here is
the need for another Commission to look after the
Health of Africa.   That, too, should be of authority
over all the area of " tutelage " Africa.   It is no
good stamping out infectious disease in Nyasaland
while it is being bred in Portuguese East Africa.
And if there is a Disarmament Commission already
controlling the importation of arms, why should
not that body also control at the same time the
importation of trade gin and similar delicacies,
and direct quarantine and such-like health regu-
lations ?

But there is another question in Africa upon
which our " ignorant " Labour class is far better
informed than our dear old eighteenth-century
upper class which still squats so firmly in our
Foreign and Colonial Offices, and that is the
question of forced labour.   We cannot tolerate

any possibilities of the enslavement of black Africa.
Long ago the United States found out the impossibility of having slave labour working in the same
system with white.   To cure that anomaly cost
the United States a long and bloody war.   The
slave-owner, the exploiter of the black, becomes
a threat and a nuisance to any white democracy.
He brings back his loot to corrupt Press and life at
home.   What happened in America in the midst
of the last century between Federals and Con-
federates must not happen again on a larger scale
between white Europe and middle Africa.   Slavery
in Africa, open or disguised, whether enforced by
the lash or brought about by iniquitous land-
stealing, strikes at the home and freedom of every
European worker—*and Labour knows this.*

But how are we to prevent the enslavement and
economic exploitation of the blacks if we have no
general watcher of African conditions ?   We want
a common law for Africa, a general Declaration of
Rights, of certain elementary rights, and we want
a common authority to which the black man and
the native tribe may appeal for justice.   What is
the good of trying to elevate the population of
Uganda and to give it a free and hopeful life if
some other population close at hand is competing
against the Baganda worker under lash and tax ?
So here is a third aspect of our international

Commission, as a native protectorate and court of appeal !

There is still a fourth aspect of the African question in which every mother's son in Europe is closely interested, and that is the trade question. Africa is the great source of many of the most necessary raw materials upon which our modern comforts and conveniences depend ; more particularly is it the source of cheap fat in the form of palm oil. One of the most powerful levers in the hands of the Allied democracies at the present time in their struggle against the imperial brigands of Potsdam is the complete control we have now obtained over these essential supplies. We can, if we choose, cut off Germany altogether from these vital economic necessities, if she does not consent to abandon militant imperialism for some more civilized form of government. We hope that this war will end in that renunciation, and that Germany will re-enter the community of nations. But whether that is so or not, whether Germany is or is not to be one of the interested parties in the African solution, the fact remains that it is impossible to contemplate a continuing struggle for the African raw material supply between the interested Powers. Sooner or later that means a renewal of war. International trade rivalry is, indeed, only war—*smouldering*. We need, and Labour demands, a fair, frank treatment of African trade, and that can only be done by some overriding regulative power, a Commission which, so far as I can see, might also be the same Commission as that we have already hypothesized as being necessary to control the Customs in order to prevent gun-running and the gin trade. That Commission might very conveniently have a voice in the administration of the great waterways of Africa (which often run through the possessions of several Powers) and in the regulation of the big railway lines and air routes that will speedily follow the conclusion of peace.

Now this I take it is the gist of the Labour proposal. This—and no more than this—is what is intended by the "international control of tropical Africa." *I do not read that phrase as abrogating existing sovereignties in Africa.* What is contemplated is a delegation of authority. Every one should know, though unhappily the badness of our history teaching makes it doubtful if every one does know, that the Federal Government of the United States of America did not begin as a sovereign Government, and has now only a very questionable sovereignty. Each State was sovereign, and each State delegated certain powers to Washington. That was the initial idea of the union. Only later did the idea of a people of the

States as a whole emerge. In the same way I understand the Labour proposal as meaning that we should delegate to an African Commission the middle African Customs, the regulation of inter-State trade, inter-State railways and waterways, quarantine and health generally, and the establishment of a Supreme Court for middle African affairs. One or two minor matters, such as the preservation of rare animals, might very well fall under the same authority.

Upon that Commission the interested nations, that is to say—putting them in alphabetical order—the Africander, the Briton, the Belgian, the Egyptian, the Frenchman, the Italian, the Indian the Portuguese—might all be represented in proportion to their interest. Whether the German would come in is really a question for the German to consider ; he can come in as a good European, he cannot come in as an imperialist brigand. Whether, too, any other nations can claim to have an interest in African affairs, whether the Commission would not be better appointed by a League of Free Nations than directly by the interested Governments, and a number of other such questions, need not be considered here. Here we are discussing only the main idea of the Labour proposal.

Now beneath the supervision and restraint of

E

such a delegated Commission I do not see why the existing administrations of tutelage Africa should not continue. I do not believe that the Labour proposal contemplates any humiliating cession of European sovereignty. Under that international Commission the French flag may still wave in Senegal and the British over the protected State of Uganda. Given a new spirit in Germany I do not see why the German flag should not presently be restored in German East Africa. But over all, standing for righteousness, patience, fair play for the black, and the common welfare of mankind would wave a new flag, the Sun of Africa representing the Central African Commission of the League of Free Nations.

That is my vision of the Labour project. It is something very different, I know, from the nightmare of an international police of cosmopolitan scoundrels in nondescript uniforms, hastening to loot and ravish his dear Uganda and his beloved Nigeria, which distresses the crumpled pillow of Sir Harry Johnston. But if it is not the solution, then it is up to him and his fellow authorities to tell us what is the solution of the African riddle.

V

GETTING THE LEAGUE IDEA CLEAR IN RELATION TO IMPERIALISM

§ 1

IT is idle to pretend that even at the present time the idea of the League of Free Nations has secure possession of the British mind. There is quite naturally a sustained opposition to it in all the fastnesses of aggressive imperialism. Such papers as the *Times* and the *Morning Post* remain hostile and obstructive to the expression of international ideas. Most of our elder statesmen seem to have learnt nothing and forgotten nothing during the years of wildest change the world has ever known. But in the general mind of the British peoples the movement of opinion from a narrow imperialism towards internationalism has been wide and swift. And it continues steadily. One can trace week by week and almost day by day the Americanization of the British conception of the Allied War Aims. It may be interesting to reproduce here three communications upon this question made at different times by the present writer to the press. The circumstances of their publication are significant. The first is in substance identical with a letter which was sent to the *Times* late in May, 1917, and rejected as being altogether too revolutionary. For nowadays the correspondence in the *Times* has ceased to be an impartial expression of public opinion. The correspondence of the *Times* is now apparently selected and edited in accordance with the views upon public policy held by the acting editor for the day. More and more has that paper become the organ of a sort of Oxford Imperialism, three or four years behind the times and very ripe and " expert." The letter is here given as it was finally printed in the issue of the *Daily Chronicle* for June 4th, 1917, under the heading, " Wanted a Statement of Imperial Policy."

Sir,—The time seems to have come for much clearer statements of outlook and intention from this country than it has hitherto been possible to make. The entry of America into the war and the banishment of autocracy and aggressive diplomacy from Russia have enormously cleared the air, and the recent great speech of General Smuts at the Savoy Hotel is probably only the first of a series of experiments in statement. It is desirable alike to clear our own heads, to unify our efforts, and to give the nations of the world some assurance and standard for our national conduct in the future, that we should now define the Idea of our Empire and its relation to the world outlook much more clearly than has ever hitherto been done. Never before in the history of mankind has opinion counted for so much and persons and organizations for so little as in this war. Never before has the need for clear ideas, widely understood and consistently sustained, been so commandingly vital.

What do we mean by our Empire, and what is its relation to that universal desire of mankind, the permanent rule of peace and justice in the world ? The whole world will be the better for a very plain answer to that question.

Is it not time for us British not merely to admit to ourselves, but to assure the world that our Empire as it exists to-day is a provisional thing, that in scarcely any part of the world do we regard it as more than an emergency arrangement, as a necessary association that must give place ultimately to the higher synthesis of a world league, that here we hold as trustees and there on account of strategic considerations that may presently disappear, and that though we will not contemplate the replacement of our flag anywhere by the flag of any other competing nation, though we do hope to hold together with our kin and with those who increasingly share our tradition and our language, nevertheless we are prepared to welcome great renunciations of our present ascendency and privileges in the interests of mankind as a whole. We need to make the world understand that we do not put our nation nor our Empire before the commonwealth of man. Unless presently we are to follow Germany along the tragic path her national vanity and her world ambitions have made for her, that is what we have to make clear now. It is not only our duty to mankind, it is also the sane course for our own preservation.

Is it not the plain lesson of this stupendous and disastrous war that there is no way to secure civilization from destruction except by an impartial control and protection in the interests of the whole human race, a control representing the best intelligence of mankind, of these main causes of war.

(1) The politically undeveloped tropics ;

(2) Shipping and international trade ; and

(3) Small nationalities and all regions in a state of political impotence or confusion ?

It is our case against the Germans that in all these three cases they have subordinated every consideration of justice and the general human welfare to a monstrous national egotism. That argument has a double edge. At present there is a vigorous campaign in America, Russia, the neutral countries generally, to represent British patriotism as equally egotistic, and our purpose in this war as a mere parallel to the German purpose. In the same manner, though perhaps with less persistency, France and Italy are also caricatured. We are supposed to be grabbing at Mesopotamia and Palestine, France at Syria; Italy is represented as pursuing a Machiavellian policy towards the unfortunate Greek republicans, with her eyes on the Greek islands and Greece in Asia. Is it not time that these base imputations were repudiated clearly and conclusively by our Alliance? And is it not time that we began to discuss in much more frank and definite terms than has hitherto been done, the nature of the international arrangement that will be needed to secure the safety of such liberated populations as those of Palestine, of the Arab regions of the old Turkish empire, of Armenia, of reunited Poland, and the like?

I do not mean here mere diplomatic discussions and "understandings," I mean such full and plain statements as will be spread through the whole world and grasped and assimilated by ordinary people everywhere, statements by which we, as a people, will be prepared to stand or fall.

Almost as urgent is the need for some definite statement about Africa. General Smuts has warned not only the Empire, but the whole world of the gigantic threat to civilization that lies in the present division of Africa between various keenly competitive European Powers, any one of which will be free to misuse the great natural resources at its disposal and to arm millions of black soldiers for aggression. A mere elimination of Germany from Africa will not solve that difficulty. What we have to eliminate is not this nation or that, but the system of national shoving and elbowing, the treatment of Africa as the board for a game of beggar-my-neighbour-and-damn-the-niggers, in which a few syndicates, masquerading as national interests, snatch a profit to the infinite loss of all mankind. We want a lowering of barriers and a unification of interests, we want an international control of these disputed regions, to override nationalist exploitation. The whole world wants it. It is a chastened and reasonable world we live in to-day, and the time for white reason and the wide treatment of these problems is now.

Finally, the time is drawing near when the Egyptian and the nations of India will ask us, "Are things going on for ever here as they go on now, or are we to look for the time when we, too, like the Africander, the Canadian and the Australian, will be your confessed and equal partners? " Would it not be wise to answer that question in the affirmative before the voice in which it is asked grows thick with anger ? In Egypt, for example, we are either robbers very like—except for a certain difference in touch—the Germans in Belgium, or we are honourable trustees. It is our claim and pride to be honourable trustees. Nothing so becomes a trustee as a cheerful openness of disposition. Great Britain has to table her world policy. It is a thing overdue. No doubt we have already a literature of liberal imperialism and a considerable accumulation of declarations by this statesman or that. But what is needed is a formulation much more representative, official and permanent than that, something that can be put beside President Wilson's clear rendering of the American idea. We want all our peoples to understand, and we want all mankind to understand that our Empire is not a net about the world in which the progress of mankind is entangled, but a self-conscious political system working side by side with the other democracies of the earth, preparing the way for, and prepared at last to sacrifice and merge itself in, the world confederation of free and equal peoples.

§ 2

This letter was presently followed up by an article in the *Daily News*, entitled " A Reasonable Man's Peace." This article provoked a considerable controversy in the imperialist press, and it was reprinted as a pamphlet by a Free Trade organization, which distributed over 200,000 copies. It is particularly interesting to note, in view of what follows it, that it was attacked with great virulence in the *Evening News*, the little fierce mud-throwing brother of the *Daily Mail*.

The international situation at the present time is beyond question the most wonderful that the world has ever seen. There is not a country in the world in which the great majority of sensible people are not passionately desirous of peace, of an enduring peace, and—the war goes on. The conditions of peace can now be stated in general terms that are as acceptable to a reasonable man in Berlin as they are to a reasonable man in Paris or London or Petrograd or Constantinople. There are to be no conquests, no domination of recalcitrant populations, no bitter insistence upon vindictive penalties, and there must be something in the nature of a world-wide League of Nations to keep the peace securely in future, to " make the world safe for democracy," and maintain international justice. To that the general mind of the world has come to-day.

Why, then, does the waste and killing go on ? Why is not the Peace Conference sitting now ?

Manifestly because a small minority of people in positions of peculiar advantage, in positions of trust and authority, and particularly the German reactionaries, prevent or delay its assembling.

The answer which seems to suffice in all the Allied countries is that the German Imperial Government—that the German Imperial Government alone—stands in the way, that its tradition is incurably a tradition of conquest and aggression, that until German militarism is overthrown, etc. Few people in the Allied countries will dispute that that is broadly true. But is it the whole and complete truth ? Is there nothing more to be done on our side ? Let us put a question that goes to the very heart of the problem. Why does the great mass of the German people still cling to its incurably belligerent Government ?

The answer to that question is not overwhelmingly difficult. The German people sticks to its militarist imperialism as Mazeppa stuck to his horse ; because it is bound to it, and the wolves pursue. The attentive student of the home and foreign propaganda literature of the German

Government will realize that the case made by German imperialism, the main argument by which it sticks to power, is this, that the Allied Governments are also imperialist, that they also aim at conquest and aggression, that for Germany the choice is world empire or downfall and utter ruin. This is the argument that holds the German people stiffly united. For most men in most countries it would be a convincing argument, strong enough to override considerations of right and wrong. I find that I myself am of this way of thinking, that whether England has done right or wrong in the past—and I have sometimes criticized my country very bitterly—I will not endure the prospect of seeing her at the foot of some victorious foreign nation. Neither will any German who matters. Very few people would respect a German who did.

But the case for the Allies is that this great argument by which, and by which alone, the German Imperial Government keeps its grip upon the German people at the present time, and keeps them facing their enemies, is untrue. The Allies declare that they do not want to destroy the German people, they do not want to cripple the German people ; they want merely to see certain gaping wounds inflicted by Germany repaired, and beyond that reasonable requirement they want nothing but to be assured, completely assured, absolutely assured, against any further aggressions on the part of Germany.

Is that true? Our leaders say so, and we believe them. We would not support them if we did not. And if it is true, have the statesmen of the Allies made it as transparently and convincingly clear to the German people as possible? That is one of the supreme questions of the present time. We cannot too earnestly examine it. Because in the answer to it lies the reason why so many men were killed yesterday on the eastern and western front, so many ships sunk, so much property destroyed, so much human energy wasted for ever upon mere destruction, and why to-morrow and the next day and the day after—through many months yet, perhaps—the same killing and destroying must still go on.

In many respects this war has been an amazing display of human inadaptability. The military history of the war has still to be written, the grim story of machinery misunderstood, improvements resisted, antiquated methods persisted in; but the broad facts are already before the public mind. After three years of war the air offensive, the only possible decisive blow, is still merely talked of. Not once nor twice only have the Western Allies had victory within their grasp—and failed to grip it. The British cavalry generals wasted the great invention of the tanks as a careless child breaks a toy. At least equally remarkable is the dragging inadaptability of European statecraft. Everywhere the failure of ministers and statesmen to rise to the urgent definite necessities of the present time is glaringly conspicuous. They seem to be incapable even of thinking how the war may be brought to an end. They seem incapable of that plain speaking to the world audience which alone can bring about a peace. They keep on with the tricks and feints of a departed age. Both on the side of the Allies and on the side of the Germans the declarations of public policy remain childishly vague and disingenuous, childishly " diplomatic." They chaffer like happy imbeciles while civilization bleeds to death. It was perhaps to be expected. Few, if any, men of over five-and-forty completely readjust themselves to changed conditions, however novel and challenging the changes may be, and nearly all the leading figures in these affairs are elderly men trained in a tradition of diplomatic ineffectiveness, and now overworked and overstrained to a pitch of complete inelasticity. They go on as if it were still 1913. Could anything be more palpably shifty and unsatisfactory, more senile, more feebly artful, than the recent utterances of the German Chancellor ? And, on our own side—

Let us examine the three leading points about

this peace business in which this jaded statecraft is most apparent.

Let the reader ask himself the following questions :—

Does he know what the Allies mean to do with the problem of Central Africa ? It is the clear common sense of the African situation that while these precious regions of raw material remain divided up between a number of competitive European imperialisms, each resolutely set upon the exploitation of its " possessions " to its own advantage and the disadvantage of the others, there can be no permanent peace in the world. There can be permanent peace in the world only when tropical and sub-tropical Africa constitute a field free to the commercial enterprise of every one irrespective of nationality, when this is no longer an area of competition between nations. This is possible only under some supreme international control. It requires no special knowledge nor wisdom to see that. A schoolboy can see it. Any one but a statesman absolutely flaccid with overstrain can see that. However difficult it may prove to work out in detail, such an international control *must* therefore be worked out. The manifest solution of the problem of the German colonies in Africa is neither to return them to her nor deprive her of them, but to give her a share in the pooled general control of mid-Africa. In that way she can be deprived of all power for political mischief in Africa without humiliation or economic injury. In that way, too, we can head off—and in no other way can we head off—the power for evil, the power of developing quarrels inherent in " imperialisms " other than German.

But has the reader any assurance that this sane solution of the African problem has the support of the Allied Governments ? At best he has only a vague persuasion. And consider how the matter looks " over there." The German Government assures the German people that the Allies intend to cut off Germany from the African supply of raw material. That would mean the practical destruction of German economic life. It is something far more vital to the mass of Germans than any question of Belgium or Alsace-Lorraine. It is, therefore, one of the ideas most potent in nerving the overstrained German people to continue their fight. Why are we, and why are the German people, not given some definite assurance in this matter ? Given reparation in Europe, is Germany to be allowed a fair share in the control and trade of a pooled and neutralized Central Africa ? Sooner or later we must come to some such arrangement. Why not state it plainly now ?

A second question is equally essential to any
really permanent settlement, and it is one upon
which these eloquent but unsatisfactory mouth-
pieces of ours turn their backs with an equal reso-
lution, and that is the fate of the Ottoman Empire.
What in plain English are we up to there ? Whatever happens, that Humpty Dumpty cannot be
put back as it was before the war. The idea of the
German imperialist, the idea of our own little band
of noisy but influential imperialist vulgarians, is
evidently a game of grab, a perilous cutting up of
these areas into jostling protectorates and spheres
of influence, from which either the Germans or the
Allies (according to the side you are on) are to be
viciously shut out. On such a basis this war is a
war to the death. Neither Germany, France,
Britain, Italy, nor Russia can live prosperously
if its trade and enterprise is shut out from this
cardinally important area. There is, therefore,
no alternative, if we are to have a satisfactory
permanent pacification of the world, but local
self-development in these regions under honestly
conceived international control of police and
transit and trade. Let it be granted that that
will be a difficult control to organize. None the
less it has to be attempted. It has to be attempted
because *there is no other way of peace.* But once
that conception has been clearly formulated, a

F

second great motive why Germany should continue fighting will have gone.

The third great issue about which there is nothing but fog and uncertainty is the so-called "War After the War," the idea of a permanent economic alliance to prevent the economic recuperation of Germany.   Upon that idea German imperialism, in its frantic effort to keep its tormented people fighting, naturally puts the utmost stress. The threat of War after the War robs the reasonable German of his last inducement to turn on his Government and insist upon peace.   Shut out from all trade, unable to buy food, deprived of raw material, peace would be as bad for Germany as war.   He will argue naturally enough and reasonably enough that he may as well die fighting as starve.   This is a far more vital issue to him than the Belgian issue or Poland or Alsace-Lorraine. Our statesmen waste their breath and slight our intelligence when these foreground questions are thrust in front of the really fundamental matters. But as the mass of sensible people in every country concerned, in Germany just as much as in France or Great Britain, know perfectly well, unimpeded trade is good for every one except a few rich adventurers, and restricted trade destroys limitless wealth and welfare for mankind to make a few private fortunes or secure an advantage for some imperialist clique. We want an end to this economic strategy, we want an end to this plotting of Governmental cliques against the general welfare. In such offences Germany has been the chief of sinners, but which among the belligerent nations can throw the first stone ? Here again the way to the world's peace, the only way to enduring peace, lies through internationalism, through an international survey of commercial treaties, through an international control of inter-State shipping and transport rates. Unless the Allied statesmen fail to understand the implications of their own general professions they mean that. But why do they not say it plainly ? Why do they not shout it so compactly and loudly that all Germany will hear and understand ? Why do they justify imperialism to Germany ? Why do they maintain a threatening ambiguity towards Germany on all these matters ?

By doing so they leave Germany no choice but a war of desperation. They underline and endorse the claim of German imperialism that this is a war for bare existence. They unify the German people. They prolong the war.

§ 3

Some weeks later I was able, at the invitation of the editor, to carry the controversy against imperialism into the *Daily Mail*, which has hitherto counted as a strictly imperialist paper. The article that follows was published in the *Daily Mail* under the heading, " Are we Sticking to the Point ?   A Discussion of War Aims."

Has this War-Aims controversy really got down to essentials ?   Is the purpose of this world conflict from first to last too complicated for brevity, or can we boil it down into a statement compact enough for a newspaper article ?

And if we can, why is there all this voluminous, uneasy, unquenchable disputation about War Aims ?

As to the first question, I would say that the gist of the dispute between the Central Powers and the world can be written easily without undue cramping in an ordinary handwriting upon a post-card.   It is the second question that needs answering.   And the reason why the second question has to be asked and answered is this, that several of the Allies, and particularly we British, are not being perfectly plain and simple-minded in our answer to the first, that there is a division among us and in our minds, and that our division is making us ambiguous in our behaviour, that it is weakening and dividing our action and strengthening and consolidating the enemy, and that unless we can drag this slurred-over division of aim and spirit into the light of day and *settle it now*, we are likely to remain double-minded to the end of the war, to split our strength while the war continues and to come out of the settlement at the end with nothing nearly worth the strain and sacrifice it has cost us.

And first, let us deal with that postcard and say what is the essential aim of the war, the aim to which all other aims are subsidiary. It is, we have heard repeated again and again by every statesman of importance in every Allied country, to defeat and destroy military imperialism, to make the world safe for ever against any such deliberate aggression as Germany prepared for forty years and brought to a climax when she crossed the Belgian frontier in 1914. We want to make anything of that kind on the part of Germany or of any other Power henceforth impossible in this world. That is our great aim. Whatever other objects may be sought in this war no responsible statesman dare claim them as anything but subsidiary to that ; one can say, in fact, this is our sole aim, our other aims being but parts of it. Better that millions should die now, we declare, than that hundreds of millions still unborn should go on living, generation after generation, under the black tyranny of this imperialist threat.

There is our common agreement. So far, at any rate, we are united. The question I would put to the reader is this : Are we all logically, sincerely, and fully carrying out the plain implications of this War Aim ?   Or are we to any extent muddling about with it in such a way as to confuse and disorganize our Allies, weaken our internal will, and strengthen the enemy ?

Now the plain meaning of this supreme declared War Aim is that we are asking Germany to alter her ways.   We are asking Germany to become a different Germany.   Either Germany has to be utterly smashed up and destroyed or else Germany has to cease to be an aggressive military imperialism.   The former alternative is dismissed by most responsible statesmen.   They declare that they do not wish to destroy the German people or the German nationality or the civilized life of Germany. I will not enlarge here upon the tedium and difficulties such an undertaking would present.   I will dismiss it as being not only impossible, but also as an insanely wicked project.   The second alternative, therefore, remains as our War Aim.   I do not see how the sloppiest reasoner can evade that.   As we do not want to kill Germany we must want to change Germany.   If we do not want to wipe Germany off the face of the earth, then we want Germany to become the prospective and trustworthy friend of her fellow nations.   And if words have any meaning at all, that is saying that we are fighting to bring about a Revolution in Germany. We want Germany to become a democratically controlled State, such as is the United States to-day, with open methods and pacific intentions, instead of remaining a clenched fist. If we can bring that about we have achieved our War Aim ; if we cannot, then this struggle has been for us only such loss and failure as humanity has never known before.

But do we, as a nation, stick closely to this clear and necessary, this only possible, meaning of our declared War Aim ? That great, clear-minded leader among the Allies, that Englishman who more than any other single man speaks for the whole English-speaking and Western-thinking community, President Wilson, has said definitely that this is his meaning. America, with him as her spokesman, is under no delusion ; she is fighting consciously for a German Revolution as the essential War Aim. We in Europe do not seem to be so lucid. I think myself we have been, and are still, fatally and disastrously not lucid. It is high time, and over, that we cleared our minds and got down to the essentials of the war. We have muddled about in blood and dirt and secondary issues long enough.

We in Britain are not clear-minded, I would point out, because we are double-minded. No good end is served by trying to ignore in the fancied

interests of " unity " a division of spirit and intention that trips us up at every step. We are, we
declare, fighting for a complete change in international methods, and we are bound to stick to the
logical consequences of that. We have placed
ourselves on the side of democratic revolution
against autocratic monarchy, and we cannot afford
to go on shilly-shallying with that choice. We cannot in these days of black or white play the part of
lukewarm friends to freedom. I will not remind
the reader here of the horrible vacillations and in-
consistencies of policy in Greece that have prolonged
the war and cost us wealth and lives beyond measure,
but President Wilson himself has reminded us pun-
gently enough and sufficiently enough of the follies
and disingenuousness of our early treatment of the
Russian Revolution. What I want to point out
here is the supreme importance of a clear lead in
this matter *now* in order that we should state our
War Aims effectively.

In every war there must be two sets of War
Aims kept in mind ; we ought to know what we
mean to do in the event of victory so complete that
we can dictate what terms we choose, and we ought
to know what, in the event of a not altogether conclusive tussle, are the minimum terms that we
should consider justified us in a discontinuance of
the tussle. Now, unless our leading statesmen are

humbugs and unless we are prepared to quarrel with America in the interests of the monarchist institutions of Europe, we should, in the event of an overwhelming victory, destroy both the Hohenzollern and Hapsburg Imperialisms, and that means, if it means anything at all and is not mere lying rhetoric, that we should insist upon Germany becoming free and democratic, that is to say, in effect if not in form republican, and upon a series of national republics, Polish, Hungarian, Serbo-Croatian, Bulgarian, and the like, in Eastern Europe, grouped together if possible into congenial groups—crowned republics it might be in some cases, in the case of the Serb for example, but in no case too much crowned—that we should join with this renascent Germany and with these thus liberalized Powers and with our Allies and with the neutrals in one great League of Free Nations, trading freely with one another, guaranteeing each other freedom, and maintaining a world-wide peace and disarmament and a new reign of law for mankind.

If that is not what we are out for, then I do not understand what we are out for ; there is dishonesty and trickery and diplomacy and foolery in the struggle, and I am no longer whole-hearted for such a half-hearted war. If after a complete victory we are to bolster up the Hohenzollerns, Hapsburgs, and their relations, set up a constellation of more cheating little subordinate kings, and reinstate that system of diplomacies and secret treaties and secret understandings, that endless drama of international threatening and plotting, that never-ending arming, that has led us after a hundred years of waste and muddle to the supreme tragedy of this war, then the world is not good enough for me and I shall be glad to close my eyes upon it. I am not alone in these sentiments. I believe that in writing thus I am writing the opinion of the great mass of reasonable British, French, Italian, Russian, and American men. I believe, too, that this is the desire also of great numbers of Germans, and that they would, if they could believe us, gladly set aside their present rulers to achieve this plain common good for mankind.

But, the reader will say, what evidence is there of any republican feeling in Germany? That is always the objection made to any reasonable discussion of the war—and as most of us are denied access to German papers, it is difficult to produce quotations; and even when one does, there are plenty of fools to suggest and believe that the entire German Press is an elaborate camouflage. Yet in the German Press there is far more criticism of militant imperialism than those who have no access to it can imagine. There is far franker criticism of militarism in Germany than there is of reactionary Toryism in this country, and it is more free to speak its mind.

That, however, is a question by the way. It is not the main thing that I have to say here. What I have to say here is that in Great Britain—I will not discuss the affairs of any of our Allies—there are groups and classes of people, not numerous, not representative, but placed in high and influential positions and capable of free and public utterance, who are secretly and bitterly hostile to this great War Aim, which inspires all the Allied peoples. These people are permitted to deny—our peculiar censorship does not hamper them—loudly and publicly that we are fighting for democracy and world freedom ; " Tosh," they say to our dead in the trenches, " you died for a mistake " ; they jeer at this idea of a League of Nations making an end to war, an idea that has inspired countless brave lads to face death and such pains and hardships as outdo even death itself ; they perplex and irritate our Allies by propounding schemes for some precious economic league of the British Empire—that is to treat all " foreigners " with a common base selfishness and stupid hatred—and they intrigue with the most reactionary forces in Russia.

These British reactionaries openly, and with perfect impunity, represent our war as a thing as mean and shameful as Germany's attack on Belgium, and they do it because generosity and justice in the world is as terrible to them as dawn is to the creatures of the night.   Our Tories blundered into this great war, not seeing whither it would take them.   In particular it is manifest now by a hundred signs that they dread the fall of monarchy in Germany and Austria.   Far rather would they make the most abject surrenders to the Kaiser than deal with a renascent Republican Germany.   The recent letter of Lord Lansdowne, urging a peace with German imperialism, was but a feeler from the pacifist side of this most un-English, and unhappily most influential, section of our public life. Lord Lansdowne's letter was the letter of a Peer who fears revolution more than national dishonour.

But it is the truculent wing of this same antidemocratic movement that is far more active. While our sons suffer and die for their comforts and conceit, these people scheme to prevent any communication between the Republican and Socialist classes in Germany and the Allied population. At any cost this class of pampered and privileged traitors intend to have peace while the Kaiser is still on his throne.   If not they face a new world —in which their part will be small indeed.   And with the utmost ingenuity they maintain a dangerous vagueness about the Allied peace terms, *with*

the sole object of preventing a revolutionary move-
ment in Germany.

Let me put it to the reader exactly why our
failure to say plainly and exactly and conclusively
what we mean to do about a score of points, and
particularly about German economic life after the
war, paralyses the penitents and friends and helpers
that we could now find in Germany. Let me ask
the reader to suppose himself a German in Germany
at the present time. Of course if he was, he is sure
that he would hate the Kaiser as the source of this
atrocious war, he would be bitterly ashamed of the
Belgian iniquity, of the submarine murders, and a
score of such stains upon his national honour ; and
he would want to alter his national system and
make peace. Hundreds of thousands of Germans
are in that mood now. But as most of us have
had to learn, a man may be bitterly ashamed of
this or that incident in his country's history—what
Englishman, for instance, can be proud of Glencoe ?
—he may disbelieve in half its institutions and still
love his country far too much to suffer the thought
of its destruction. I prefer to see my country
right, but if it comes to the pinch and my country
sins I will fight to save her from the destruction her
sins may have brought upon her. That is the
natural way of a man.

But suppose a German wished to try to start a

revolutionary movement in Germany at the present time, have we given him any reason at all for supposing that a Germany liberated and democratized, but, of course, divided and weakened as she would be bound to be in the process, would get better terms from the Allies than a Germany still facing them, militant, imperialist, and wicked ?   He would have no reason for believing anything of the sort. If we Allies are honest, then if a revolution started in Germany to-day we should if anything lower the price of peace to Germany.   But these people who pretend to lead us will state nothing of the sort. For them a revolution in Germany would be the signal for putting up the price of peace.   At any risk they are resolved that that German revolution shall not happen.   Your sane, good German, let me assert, is up against that as hard as if he was a wicked one.   And so, poor devil, he has to put his revolutionary ideas away, they are hopeless ideas for him because of the power of the British reactionary, they are hopeless because of the line we as a nation take in this matter, and he has to go on fighting for his masters.

A plain statement of our war aims that did no more than set out honestly and convincingly the terms the Allies would make with a democratic republican Germany—republican I say, because where a scrap of Hohenzollern is left to-day there will be a fresh militarism to-morrow—would absolutely revolutionize the internal psychology of Germany. We should no longer face a solid people. We should have replaced the false issue of Germany and Britain fighting for the hegemony of Europe, the lie upon which the German Government has always traded, and in which our extreme Tory Press has always supported the German Government, by the true issue, which is freedom versus imperialism, the League of Nations versus that net of diplomatic roguery and of aristocratic, plutocratic, and autocratic greed and conceit which dragged us all into this vast welter of bloodshed and loss.

VI

THE WAR AIMS OF THE WESTERN ALLIES

HERE, quite compactly, is the plain statement of the essential cause and process of the war to which I would like to see the Allied Foreign Offices subscribe, and which I would like to have placed plainly before the German mind. It embodies much that has been learnt and thought out since this war began, and I think it is much truer and more fundamental than that mere raging against German "militarism," upon which our politicians and press still so largely subsist.

The enormous development of war methods and war material within the last fifty years has made war so horrible and destructive that it is impossible to contemplate a future for mankind from which it has not been eliminated; the increased facilities of railway, steamship, automobile travel and air navigation have brought mankind so close together that ordinary human life is no longer safe anywhere in the boundaries of the little states in which it was once secure. In some fashion it is now necessary to achieve sufficient human unity to establish a world peace and save the future of mankind.

In one or other of two ways only is that unification possible. Either men may set up a common league to keep the peace of the earth, or one state must ultimately become so great and powerful as to repeat for all the world what Rome did for Europe two thousand years ago. Either we must have human unity by a league of existing states or by an Imperial Conquest. The former is now the declared Aim of our country and its Allies; the latter is manifestly the ambition of the present rulers of Germany. Whatever the complications may have been in the earlier stages of the war, due to treaties that are now dead letters and agreements that are extinct, the essential issue now before every man in the world is this : Is the unity of mankind to be the unity of a common freedom, in which every race and nationality may participate with complete self-respect, playing its part, according to its character, in one great world community, or is it to be reached—and it can only be so reached through many generations of bloodshed and struggle still, even if it can be ever reached in this way at all —through conquest and a German hegemony ?

While the rulers of Germany to-day are more openly aggressive and imperialist than they were

in August, 1914, the Allies arrayed against them
have made great progress in clearing up and realizing the instincts and ideals which brought them
originally into the struggle. The German government offers the world to-day a warring future in
which Germany alone is to be secure and powerful
and proud. *Mankind will not endure that.* The
Allies offer the world more and more definitely the
scheme of an organized League of Free Nations,
a rule of law and justice about the earth. To fight
for that and for no other conceivable end, the
United States of America, with the full sympathy
and co-operation of every state in the western
hemisphere, has entered the war. The British
Empire, in the midst of the stress of the great war,
has set up in Dublin a Convention of Irishmen of
all opinions with the fullest powers of deciding
upon the future of their country. If Ireland were
not divided against herself she could be free and
equal with England to-morrow. It is the open
intention of Great Britain to develop representative
government, where it has not hitherto existed, in
India and Egypt, to go on steadfastly increasing
the share of the natives of these countries in the
government of their own lands, until they too
become free and equal members of the world league.
Neither France nor Italy nor Britain nor America
has ever tampered with the shipping of other

countries except in time of war, and the trade of the British Empire has been impartially open to all the world. The extra-national " possessions," the so-called " subject nations " in the Empires of Britain, France, Italy, and Japan, are, in fact, possessions held in trust against the day when the League of Free Nations will inherit for mankind.

Is it to be union by conquest or is it to be union by league ? For any sort of man except the German the question is, Will you be a free citizen or will you be an underling to the German imperialism ? For the German now the question is a far graver and more tragic one. For him it is this : " You belong to a people not now increasing very rapidly, a numerous people, but not so numerous as some of the great peoples of the world, a people very highly trained, very well drilled and well armed, perhaps as well trained and drilled and equipped as ever it will be. The collapse of Russian imperialism has made you safe if now you can get peace, and you *can* get a peace now that will neither destroy you nor humiliate you nor open up the prospect of fresh wars. The Allies offer you such a peace. To accept it, we must warn you plainly, means refusing to go on with the manifest intentions of your present rulers, which are to launch you and your children and your children's children upon a career of struggle for war predominance, which may no doubt inflict untold deprivations and miseries upon the rest of mankind, but whose end in the long run, for Germany and things German, can be only Judgment and Death."

In such terms as these the Oceanic Allies could now state their war-will and carry the world straightway into a new phase of human history. They could but they do not. For alas! not one of them is free from the entanglements of past things; when we look for the wisdom of statesmen we find the cunning of politicians; when open speech and plain reason might save the world, courts, bureaucrats, financiers and profiteers conspire.

VII

THE FUTURE OF MONARCHY

From the very outset of this war it was manifest to the clear-headed observer that only the complete victory of German imperialism could save the dynastic system in Europe from the fate that it had challenged. That curious system had been the natural and unplanned development of the political complications of the seventeenth and eighteenth centuries. Two systems of monarchies, the Bourbon system and the German, then ruled Europe between them. With the latter was associated the tradition of the European unity under the Roman empire; all the Germanic monarchs had an itch to be called Caesar. The Kaiser of the Austro-Hungarian empire and the Czar had, so to speak, the prior claim to the title. The Prussian king set up as a Caesar in 1871; Queen Victoria became the Caesar of India (Kaisir-i-Hind) under the auspices of Lord Beaconsfield, and last and least, that most detestable of all Coburgers, Ferdinand of Bulgaria, gave Kaiserism a touch of quaint absurdity by setting up as Czar of Bulgaria. The weakening of the Bourbon system by the French revolution and the Napoleonic adventure cleared the way for the complete ascendancy of the Germanic monarchies in spite of the breaking away of the United States from that system.

After 1871, a constellation of quasi-divine Teutonic monarchs, of which the German Emperor, the German Queen Victoria, the German Czar, were the greatest stars, formed a caste apart, inter-married only among themselves, dominated the world and was regarded with a mystical awe by the ignorant and foolish in most European countries. The marriages, the funerals, the coronations, the obstetrics of this amazing breed of idols were matters of almost universal worship. The Czar and Queen Victoria professed also to be the heads of religion upon earth. The court-centered diplomacies of the more firmly rooted monarchies steered all the great liberating movements of the nineteenth century into monarchical channels. Italy was made a monarchy; Greece, the motherland of republics, was handed over to a needy scion of the Danish royal family; the sturdy peasants of Bulgaria suffered from a kindred imposition. Even Norway was saddled with as much of a king as it would stand, as a condition of its independence. At the dawn of the twentieth century republican

freedom seemed a remote dream beyond the con-
fines of Switzerland and France—and it had no
very secure air in France. Reactionary scheming
has been an intermittent fever in the French
republic for six and forty years. The French
foreign office is still undemocratic in tradition
and temper. But for the restless disloyalty of the
Hohenzollerns this German kingly caste might be
dominating the world to this day.

Of course the stability of this Teutonic dynastic
system in Europe—which will presently seem to
the student of history so curious a halting-place
upon the way to human unity—rested very largely
upon the maintenance of peace. It was the failure
to understand this on the part of the German and
Bulgarian rulers in particular that has now brought
all monarchy to the question. The implicit theory
that supported the intermarrying German royal
families in Europe was that their inter-relationship
and their aloofness from their subjects was a miti-
gation of national and racial animosities. In the
days when Queen Victoria was the grandmother
of Europe this was a plausible argument. King,
Czar and Emperor, or Emperor and Emperor
would meet, and it was understood that these
meetings were the lubrication of European affairs.
The monarchs married largely, conspicuously, and
very expensively for our good. Royal funerals,

marriages, christenings, coronations, and jubilees interrupted traffic and stimulated trade everywhere. They seemed to give a *raison d'être* for mankind. It is the Emperor William and the Czar Ferdinand who have betrayed not only humanity but their own strange caste by shattering all these pleasant illusions. The wisdom of Kant is justified, and we know now that kings cause wars. It needed the shock of the great war to bring home the wisdom of that old Scotchman of Königsberg to the mind of the ordinary man. Moreover in support of the dynastic system was the fact that it did exist as the system in possession, and all prosperous and intelligent people are chary of disturbing existing things. Life is full of vestigial structures, and it is a long way to logical perfection. Let us keep on, they would argue, with what we have. And another idea which, rightly or wrongly, made men patient with the emperors and kings was an exaggerated idea of the insecurity of republican institutions.

You can still hear very old dull men say gravely that " kings are better than pronunciamentos " ; there was an article upon Greece to this effect quite recently in that uncertain paper *The New Statesman*. Then a kind of illustrative gesture would be made to the South American republics, although the internal disturbances of the South American

republics have diminished to very small dimensions
in the last three decades and although pronunciamentos rarely disturb the traffic in Switzerland, the
United States, or France. But there can be no
doubt that the influence of the Germanic monarchy
up to the death of Queen Victoria upon British
thought was in the direction of estrangement from
the two great modern republics and in the direction of assistance and propitiation to Germany.
We surrendered Heligoland, we made great concessions to German colonial ambitions, we allowed
ourselves to be jockeyed into a phase of dangerous
hostility to France. A practice of sneering at
things American has died only very recently out
of English journalism and literature, as any one
who cares to consult the bound magazines of the
'seventies and 'eighties may soon see for himself.
It is well too in these days not to forget Colonel
Marchand, if only to remember that such a clash
must never recur. But in justice to our monarchy
we must remember that after the death of Queen
Victoria, the spirit, if not the forms, of British
kingship was greatly modified by the exceptional
character and ability of King Edward VII. He
was curiously anti-German in spirit ; he had essentially democratic instincts ; in a few precious years
he restored good will between France and Great
Britain. It is no slight upon his successor to

doubt whether any one could have handled the present opportunities and risks of monarchy in Great Britain as Edward could have handled them.

Because no doubt if monarchy is to survive in the British Empire it must speedily undergo the profoundest modification. The old state of affairs cannot continue. The European dynastic system, based upon the intermarriage of a group of mainly German royal families, is dead to-day ; it is freshly dead, but it is as dead as the rule of the Incas. It is idle to close our eyes to this fact. The revolution in Russia, the setting up of a republic in China, demonstrating the ripeness of the East for free institutions, the entry of the American republics into world politics—these things slam the door on any idea of working back to the old nineteenth-century system. People calls to people. " No peace with the Hohenzollerns " is a cry that carries with it the final repudiation of emperors and kings. The man in the street will assure you he wants no diplomatic peace. Beyond the unstable shapes of the present the political forms of the future rise now so clearly that they are the common talk of men. Kant's lucid thought told us long ago that the peace of the world demanded a world union of republics. That is a commonplace remark now in every civilized community.

The stars in their courses, the logic of circumstances, the everyday needs and everyday intelligence of men, all these things march irresistibly towards a permanent world peace based on democratic republicanism. The question of the future of monarchy is not whether it will be able to resist and overcome that trend; it has as little chance of doing that as the Lama of Thibet has of becoming Emperor of the Earth. It is whether it will resist openly, become the centre and symbol of a reactionary resistance, and have to be abolished and swept away altogether everywhere, as the Romanoffs have already been swept away in Russia, or whether it will be able in this country and that to adapt itself to the necessities of the great age that dawns upon mankind, to take a generous and helpful attitude towards its own modification, and so survive, for a time at any rate, in that larger air.

It is the fashion for the apologists of monarchy in the British Empire to speak of the British system as a crowned republic. That is an attractive phrase to people of republican sentiments. It is quite conceivable that the British Empire may be able to make that phrase a reality and that the royal line may continue, a line of hereditary presidents, with some of the ancient trappings and something of the picturesque prestige that, as the oldest monarchy in Europe, it has to-day. Two kings in Europe have already gone far towards realizing this conception of a life president; both the King of Italy and the King of Norway live as simply as if they were in the White House and are far more accessible. Along that line the British monarchy must go if it is not to go altogether. Will it go along those lines?

There are many reasons for hoping that it will do so. The *Times* has styled the crown the " golden link " of the empire. Australians and Canadians, it was argued, had little love for the motherland but the greatest devotion to the sovereign, and still truer was this of Indians, Egyptians, and the like. It might be easy to press this theory of devotion too far, but there can be little doubt that the British Crown does at present stand as a symbol of unity over diversity such as no other crown, unless it be that of Austria-Hungary, can be said to do. The British crown is not like other crowns; it may conceivably take a line of its own and emerge—possibly a little more like a hat and a little less like a crown—from trials that may destroy every other monarchial system in the world.

Now many things are going on behind the scenes, many little indications peep out upon the speculative watcher and vanish again; but there is very little that is definite to go upon at the present time to determine how far the monarchy will rise to the needs of this great occasion. Certain acts and changes, the initiative to which would come most gracefully from royalty itself, could be done at this present time. They may be done quite soon. Upon the doing of them wait great masses of public opinion. The first of these things is for the British monarchy to sever itself definitely from the German dynastic system with which it is so fatally entangled by marriage and descent, and to make its intention of becoming henceforth more and more British in blood as well as spirit, unmistakably plain. This idea has been put forth quite prominently in the *Times*. The king has been asked to give his countenance to the sweeping away of all those restrictions first set up by George the Third, upon the marriage of the Royal Princes with British, French and American subjects. The British Empire is very near the limit of its endurance of a kingly caste of Germans. The choice of British royalty between its peoples and its cousins cannot be indefinitely delayed. Were it made now publicly and boldly, there can be no doubt that the decision would mean a renascence of monarchy, a considerable outbreak of royalist enthusiasm in the Empire. There are times when a king or queen must need be dramatic and must a little anticipate occasions. It is not seemly to make concessions perforce ; kings may not make obviously unwilling surrenders ; it is the indecisive kings who lose their crowns.

No doubt the Anglicization of the royal family by national marriages would gradually merge that family into the general body of the British peerage. Its consequent loss of distinction might be accompanied by an associated fading out of function, until the King became at last hardly more functional than was the late Duke of Norfolk as premier peer. Possibly that is the most desirable course from many points of view.

It must be admitted that the abandonment of marriages within the royal caste and a bold attempt to introduce a strain of British blood in the royal family does not in itself fulfil all that is needed if the British king is indeed to become the crowned president of his people and the nominal and accepted leader of the movement towards republican institutions. A thing that is productive of an enormous amount of republican talk in Great Britain is the suspicion—I believe an ill-founded suspicion —that there are influences at work at court antagonistic to republican institutions in friendly states and that there is a disposition even to sacrifice the interests of the liberal allies to dynastic sympathies. These things are not to be believed, but it would be a feat of vast impressiveness if there were something like a royal and public repudiation of the weaknesses of cousinship. The behaviour of the Allies towards that great Balkan statesman Venizelos, the sacrificing of the friendly Greek republicans in favour of the manifestly treacherous King of Greece, has produced the deepest shame and disgust in many quarters that are altogether friendly, that are even warmly "loyal" to the British monarchy.

And in a phase of tottering thrones it is very undesirable that the British habit of asylum should be abused. We have already in England the dethroned monarch of a friendly republic; he is no doubt duly looked after. In the future there may be a shaking of the autumnal boughs and a shower of emperors and kings. We do not want Great Britain to become a hotbed of reactionary plotting and the starting-point of restoration raids into the territories of emancipated peoples. This is particularly desirable if presently, after the Kaiser's death—which by all the statistics of Hohenzollern mortality cannot be delayed now for many years—the present Crown Prince goes a-wandering. We do not want any German ex-monarchs; Sweden is always open to them and friendly, and to Sweden they ought to go; and particularly do British people dread an irruption of Hohenzollerns or Coburgers. Almost as undesirable would be the arrival of the Czar and Czarina. It is supremely important that no wind of suspicion should blow between us and the freedom of Russia. After the war even more than during the war will the enemy be anxious to sow discord between the great Russian-speaking and English-speaking democracies. Quite apart from the scandal of their inelegant domesticities, the establishment of the Czar and Czarina in England with frequent and easy access to our royal family may be extraordinarily unfortunate for the British monarchy. I will confess a certain sympathy for the Czar myself. He is not an evil figure, he is not a strong figure, but he has that sort of weakness, that failure in decision, which trails revolution in its wake. He has ended one dynasty already. The British royal family owes it to itself, that he bring not the infection of his misfortunes to Windsor.

The security of the British monarchy lies in such a courageous severance of its destinies from the Teutonic dynastic system. Will it make that severance? There I share an almost universal ignorance. The loyalty of the British is not to what kings are too prone to call " my person," not to a chosen and admired family, but to a renascent mankind. We have fought in this war for Belgium, for France, for general freedom, for civilization and the whole future of mankind, far more than for ourselves. We have not fought for a king. We are discovering in that spirit of human unity that lies below the idea of a League of Free Nations the real invisible king of our heart and race. But we will very gladly go on with our task under a nominal king unless he hampers us in the task that grows ever more plainly before us. . . . That, I think, is a fair statement of British public opinion on this question. But every day when I am in London I walk past Buckingham Palace to lunch at my club, and I look at that not very expressive façade and wonder—and we all wonder—what thoughts are going on behind it and what acts are being conceived there. Out of it there might yet come some gesture of acceptance magnificent enough to set beside President Wilson's magnificent declaration of war. . . .

These are things in the scales of fate. I will not pretend to be able to guess even which way the scales will swing.

VIII

THE PLAIN NECESSITY FOR A LEAGUE

GREAT as the sacrifices of prejudice and pre-conception which any effective realization of this idea of a League of Free Nations will demand, difficult as the necessary delegations of sovereignty must be, none the less are such sacrifices and difficulties unavoidable. People in France and Italy and Great Britain and Germany alike have to subdue their minds to the realization that some such League is now a necessity for them if their peace and national life are to continue. There is no prospect before them but either some such League or else great humiliation and disastrous warfare driving them down towards social dissolution; and for the United States it is only a question of a little longer time before the same alternatives have to be faced.

Whether this war ends in the complete defeat of Germany and German imperialism, or in a revolutionary modernization of Germany, or in a practical triumph for the Hohenzollerns, are considerations that affect the nature and scope of the

League, but do not affect its essential necessity. In the first two cases the League of Free Nations will be a world league including Germany as a principal partner, in the latter case the League of Free Nations will be a defensive league standing steadfast against the threat of a world imperialism, and watching and restraining with one common will the homicidal maniac in its midst. But in all these cases there can be no great alleviation of the evils that now blacken and threaten to ruin human life altogether, unless all the civilized and peace-seeking peoples of the world are pledged and locked together under a common law and a common world policy. There must rather be an intensification of these evils. There must be wars more evil than this war continuing this war, and more destructive of civilized life. There can be no peace and hope for our race but an organized peace and hope, armed against disturbance as a state is armed against mad, ferocious, and criminal men.

Now, there are two chief arguments, running one into the other, for the necessity of merging our existing sovereignties into a greater and, if possible, a world-wide league. The first is the present geographical impossibility of nearly all the existing European states and empires; and the second is the steadily increasing disproportion between the tortures and destructions inflicted by modern warfare and any possible advantages that may arise from it. Underlying both arguments is the fact that modern developments of mechanical science have brought the nations of Europe together into too close a proximity. This present war, more than anything else, is a violent struggle between old political ideas and new antagonistic conditions.

It is the unhappy usage of our schools and universities to study the history of mankind only during periods of mechanical unprogressiveness. The historical ideas of Europe range between the time when the Greeks were going about the world on foot or horseback or in galleys or sailing ships to the days when Napoleon, Wellington, and Nelson were going about at very much the same pace in much the same vehicles and vessels. At the advent of steam and electricity the muse of history holds her nose and shuts her eyes. Science will study and get the better of a modern disease, as, for example, sleeping sickness, in spite of the fact that it has no classical standing; but our history schools would be shocked at the bare idea of studying the effect of modern means of communication upon administrative areas, large or small. This defect in our historical training has made our minds politically sluggish. We fail to adapt readily enough. In small things and great alike we are trying to run the world in areas marked out in or before the eighteenth century, regardless of the fact that a man or an army or an aeroplane can get in a few minutes or a few hours to points that it would have taken days or weeks to reach under the old foot-and-horse conditions. That matters nothing to the learned men who instruct our statesmen and politicians. It matters everything from the point of view of social and economic and political life. And the grave fact to consider is that all the great states of Europe, except for the unification of Italy and Germany, are still much of the size and in much the same boundaries that made them strong and safe in the eighteenth century, that is to say, in the closing years of the foot-horse period. The British empire grew and was organized under those conditions, and had to modify itself only a little to meet the needs of steam shipping. All over the world are its linked possessions and its ports and coaling stations and fastnesses on the trade routes. And British people still look at the red-splashed map of the world with the profoundest self-satisfaction, blind to the swift changes that are making that scattered empire—if it is to remain an isolated system— almost the most dangerous conceivable.

Let me ask the British reader who is disposed to sneer at the League of Nations and say he is very well content with the empire, thank you, to get his atlas and consider one or two propositions. And, first, let him think of aviation. I can assure him, because upon this matter I have some special knowledge, that long-distance air travel for men, for letters and light goods and for bombs, is continually becoming more practicable. But the air routes that air transport will follow must go over a certain amount of land, for this reason that every few hundred miles at the longest the machine must come down for petrol. A flying machine with a safe non-stop range of 1500 miles is still a long way off. It may indeed be permanently impracticable because there seems to be an upward limit to the size of an aeroplane engine. And now will the reader take the map of the world and study the air routes from London to the rest of the empire? He will find them perplexing—if he wants them to be "All-Red." Happily this is not a British difficulty only. Will he next study the air routes from Paris to the rest of the French possessions? And, finally, will he study the air routes out of Germany to anywhere? The Germans are as badly off as any people. But we are all badly off. So far as world air transit goes any country can, if it chooses, choke any adjacent country. Directly any trade difficulty breaks out, any country can begin a vexatious campaign against its neighbour's air traffic. It can oblige it to alight at the frontier, to follow prescribed routes, to land at specified places on those routes and undergo examinations that will waste precious hours. But so far as I can see, no European statesman, German or Allied, have begun to give their attention to this amazing difficulty. Without a great pooling of air control, either a world-wide pooling or a pooling at least of the Atlantic-Mediterranean Allies in one Air League, the splendid peace possibilities of air transport—and they are indeed splendid—must remain very largely a forbidden possibility to mankind.

And as a second illustration of the way in which changing conditions are altering political questions, let the reader take his atlas and consider the case of that impregnable fastness, that great naval station, that Key to the Mediterranean, Gibraltar. British boys are brought up on Gibraltar and the Gibraltar idea. To the British imagination Gibraltar is almost as sacred a national symbol as the lions in Trafalgar Square. Now, in his atlas the reader will almost certainly find an inset map of this valuable possession, coloured bright red. The inset map will have attached to it a small scale of miles. From that he will be able to satisfy himself that there is not an inch of the rock anywhere that is not within five miles or less of Spanish land, and that there is rather more than a semicircle of hills round the rock within a range of seven or eight miles. That is much less than the range of a sixteen-inch gun. In other words, the Spaniards are in a position to knock Gibraltar to bits whenever they want to do so, or to smash and sink any ships in its harbour. They can hit it on every side. Consider, moreover, that there are long sweeps of coast north, south, and west of the Rock, from which torpedoes could be discharged at any ship that approached. Inquire further where on the Rock an aeroplane can land. And having ascertained these things, ask yourself what is the present value of Gibraltar ?

I will not multiply disagreeable instances of this sort, though it would be easy enough to do so in the case both of France and Italy as well as of Great Britain. I give them as illustrations of the way in which everywhere old securities and old arrangements must be upset by the greater range of modern things. Let us get on to more general conditions. There is not a capital city in Europe that twenty years from now will not be liable to a bombing raid done by hundreds or even thousands of big aeroplanes, upon or even before a declaration of war, and there is not a line of sea communication that will not be as promptly interrupted by the hostile submarine. I point these things out here

only to carry home the fact that the ideas of
sovereign isolation and detachment that were
perfectly valid in 1900, the self-sufficient empire,
Imperial Zollverein and all that stuff, and damn
the foreigner ! are now, because of the enormous
changes in range of action and facility of locomotion
that have been going on, almost as wild—or would
be if we were not so fatally accustomed to them—
and quite as dangerous, as the idea of setting up
a free and sovereign state in the Isle of Dogs.   All
the European empires are becoming vulnerable
at every point. Surely the moral is obvious.
The only wise course before the allied European
powers now is to put their national conceit in their
pockets and to combine to lock up their foreign
policy, their trade interests, and all their imperial
and international interests into a League so big
as to be able to withstand the most sudden and
treacherous of blows. And surely the only completely safe course for them and mankind—hard
and nearly impossible though it may seem at the
present juncture—is for them to lock up into one
unity with a democratized Germany and with all
the other states of the earth into one peace-main-
taining League.

If the reader will revert again to his atlas he
will see very clearly that a strongly consolidated
League of Free Nations, even if it consisted only

of our present allies, would in itself form a combination with so close a system of communication about the world, and so great an economic advantage, that in the long run it could oblige Germany and the rest of the world to come in to its council. Divided the Oceanic Allies are, to speak plainly, geographical rags and nakedness; united they are a world. To set about organizing that League now, with its necessary repudiation on the part of Britain, France, and Italy, of a selfish and, it must be remembered in the light of these things I have but hinted at here, a *now hopelessly unpracticable imperialism*, would, I am convinced, lead quite rapidly to a great change of heart in Germany and to a satisfactory peace. But even if I am wrong in that, then all the stronger is the reason for binding, locking and uniting the allied powers together. It is the most dangerous of delusions for each and all of them to suppose that either Britain, France or Italy can ever stand alone again and be secure.

And turning now to the other aspect of these consequences of the development of material science, it is too often assumed that this war is being as horrible and destructive as war can be. There never was so great a delusion. This war has only begun to be horrible. No doubt it is much more horrible and destructive than any former war, but even in comparison with the full possibilities of known and existing means of destruction it is still a mild war. Perhaps it will never rise to its full possibilities. At the present stage there is not a combatant, except perhaps America, which is not now practising a pinching economy of steel and other mechanical material. The Germans are running short of first-class flying men, and if we and our allies continue to press the air attack, and seek out and train our own vastly greater resources of first quality young airmen, the Germans may come as near to being " driven out of the air " as is possible. I am a firmer believer than ever I was in the possibility of a complete victory over Germany—through and by the air. But the occasional dropping of a big bomb or so in London is not to be taken as anything but a minimum display of what air war can do. In a little while now our alliance should be in a position to commence day and night continuous attacks upon the Rhine towns. Not hour-long raids such as London knows, but week-long raids. Then and then only shall we be able to gauge the really horrible possibilities of the air war. They are in our hands and not in the hands of the Germans. In addition the Germans are at a huge disadvantage in their submarine campaign. Their submarine campaign is only the feeble shadow of what a submarine campaign might be. Turning again to the atlas the reader can see for himself that the German and Austrian submarines are obliged to come out across very narrow fronts. A fence of mines less than three hundred miles long and two hundred feet deep would, for example, completely bar their exit through the North Sea. The U-boats run the gauntlet of that long narrow sea and pay a heavy toll to it. If only our Admiralty would tell the German public what that toll is now, there would come a time when German seamen would no longer consent to go down in them. Consider, however, what a submarine campaign would be for Great Britain if instead of struggling through this bottle-neck it were conducted from the coast of Norway, where these pests might harbour in a hundred fiords. Consider too what this weapon may be in twenty years' time in the hands of a country in the position of the United States. Great Britain, if she is not altogether mad, will cease to be an island as soon as possible after the war, by piercing the Channel Tunnel—how different our transport problem would be if we had that now!—but such countries as Australia, New Zealand, and Japan, directly they are involved in the future in a war against any efficient naval power with an unimpeded sea access, will be isolated forthwith. I cannot conceive that any of the great ocean powers will

rest content until such a tremendous possibility
of blockade as the submarine has created is
securely vested in the hands of a common league
beyond any power of sudden abuse.

It must always be remembered that this war
is a mechanical war conducted by men whose
discipline renders them uninventive, who know
little or nothing of mechanism, who are for the
most part struggling blindly to get things back
to the conditions for which they were trained, to
Napoleonic conditions, with infantry and cavalry
and comparatively light guns, the so-called " war
of manœuvres." It is like a man engaged in a
desperate duel who keeps on trying to make it a
game of cricket. Most of these soldiers detest
every sort of mechanical device ; the tanks,
for example, which, used with imagination, might
have given the British and French overwhelming
victory on the western front, were subordinated
to the usual cavalry " break through " idea. I am
not making any particular complaint against the
British and French generals in saying this. It is
what must happen to any country which entrusts
its welfare to soldiers. A soldier has to be a
severely disciplined man, and a severely disciplined
man cannot be a versatile man, and on the whole
the British army has been as receptive to novelties
as any. The German generals have done no better ;

indeed, they have not done so well as the generals of the Allies in this respect. But after the war, if the world does not organize rapidly for peace, then as resources accumulate a little, the mechanical genius will get to work on the possibilities of these ideas that have merely been sketched out in this war. We shall get big land ironclads which will smash towns. We shall get air offensives—let the experienced London reader think of an air raid going on hour after hour, day after day—that will really burn out and wreck towns, that will drive people mad by the thousand. We shall get a very complete cessation of sea transit. Even land transit may be enormously hampered by aerial attack. I doubt if any sort of social order will really be able to stand the strain of a fully worked out modern war. We have still, of course, to feel the full shock effects even of this war. Most of the combatants are going on, as sometimes men who have incurred grave wounds will still go on for a time—without feeling them. The educational, biological, social, economic punishment that has already been taken by each of the European countries is, I feel, very much greater than we yet realize. Russia, the heaviest and worst-trained combatant, has indeed shown the effects and is down and sick, but in three years' time all Europe will know far better than it does now the full price of this war. And the shock effects of the next war will have much the same relation to the shock effects of this, as the shock of breaking a finger-nail has to the shock of crushing in a body. In Russia to-day we have seen, not indeed social revolution, not the replacement of one social order by another, but disintegration. Let not national conceit blind us. Germany, France, Italy, Britain are all slipping about on that same slope down which Russia has slid. Which goes first, it is hard to guess, or whether we shall all hold out to some kind of Peace. At present the social discipline of France and Britain seems to be at least as good as that of Germany, and the *morale* of the Rhineland and Bavaria has probably to undergo very severe testing by systematized and steadily increasing air punishment as this year goes on. The next war—if a next war comes—will see all Germany, from end to end, vulnerable to aircraft. . . .

Such are the two sets of considerations that will, I think, ultimately prevail over every prejudice and every difficulty in the way of the League of Free Nations. Existing states have become impossible as absolutely independent sovereignties. The new conditions bring them so close together and give them such extravagant powers of mutual injury that they must either sink national pride and dynastic ambitions in subordination to the common welfare of mankind or else utterly shatter one another. It becomes more and more plainly a choice between the League of Free Nations and a famished race of men looting in search of non-existent food amidst the smouldering ruins of civilization. In the end I believe that the common sense of mankind will prefer a revision of its ideas of nationality and imperialism, to the latter alternative. It may take obstinate men a few more years yet of blood and horror to learn this lesson, but for my own part I cherish an obstinate belief in the potential reasonableness of mankind.

IX

DEMOCRACY

ALL the talk, all the aspiration and work that is making now towards this conception of a world securely at peace, under the direction of a League of Free Nations, has interwoven with it an idea that is often rather felt than understood, the idea of Democracy. Not only is justice to prevail between race and race and nation and nation, but also between man and man ; there is to be a universal respect for human life throughout the earth ; the world, in the words of President Wilson, is to be made " safe for democracy." I would like to subject that word to a certain scrutiny to see whether the things we are apt to think and assume about it correspond exactly with the feeling of the word. I would like to ask what, under modern conditions, does democracy mean, and whether we have got it now anywhere in the world in its fulness and completion.

And to begin with I must have a quarrel with the word itself. The eccentricities of modern education make us dependent for a number of our primary political terms upon those used by the thinkers of the small Greek republics of ancient times before those petty states collapsed, through sheer political ineptitude, before the Macedonians. They thought in terms of states so small that it was possible to gather all the citizens together for the purposes of legislation. These states were scarcely more than what we English might call sovereign urban districts. Fast communications were made by runners ; even the policeman with a bicycle of the modern urban district was beyond the scope of the Greek imagination. There were no railways, telegraphs, telephones, books or newspapers, there was no need for the state to maintain a system of education, and the affairs of the state were so simple that they could be discussed and decided by the human voice and open voting in an assembly of all the citizens. That is what democracy meant. In Andorra, or perhaps in Canton Uri, such democracy may still be possible ; in any other modern state it cannot exist. The opposite term to it was oligarchy, in which a small council of men controlled the affairs of the state. Oligarchy, narrowed down to one man, became monarchy. If you wished to be polite to an oligarchy you called it an aristocracy ; if you wished to point out that a monarch was rather by way of being self-appointed, you called him a Tyrant. An oligarchy with a property qualification was a plutocracy.

Now the modern intelligence, being under a sort of magic slavery to the ancient Greeks, has to adapt all these terms to the problems of states so vast and complex that they have the same relation to the Greek states that the anatomy of a man has to the anatomy of a jellyfish. They are not only greater in extent and denser in population, but they are increasingly innervated by more and more rapid means of communication and excitement. In the classical past—except for such special cases as the feeding of Rome with Egyptian corn—trade was a traffic in luxuries or slaves, war a small specialized affair of infantry and horsemen in search of slaves and loot, and empire the exaction of tribute. The modern state must conduct its enormous businesses through a system of ministries ; its vital interests go all round the earth ; nothing that any ancient Greek would have recognized as democracy is conceivable in a great modern state. It is absolutely necessary, if we are to get things clear in our minds about what democracy really means in relation to modern politics, first to make a quite fresh classification in order to find what items there really are to consider, and then to inquire which seem to correspond more or less closely in spirit with our ideas about ancient democracy.

Now there are two primary classes of idea about government in the modern world depending upon our conception of the political capacity of the common man. We may suppose he is a microcosm, with complete ideas and wishes about the state and the world, or we may suppose that he isn't. We may believe that the common man can govern, or we may believe that he can't. We may think further along the first line that he is so wise and good and right that we only have to get out of his way for him to act rightly and for the good of all mankind, or we may doubt it. And if we doubt that we may still believe that, though perhaps " you can fool all the people some of the time, and some of the people all the time," the common man, expressing himself by a majority vote, still remains the secure source of human wisdom. But next, while we may deny this universal distribution of political wisdom, we may, if we are sufficiently under the sway of modern ideas about collective psychology, believe that it is necessary to poke up the political indifference and inability of the common man as much as possible, to thrust political ideas and facts upon him, to incite him to a watchful and critical attitude towards them, and above all to secure his assent to the proceedings of the able people who are managing public affairs. Or finally, we may treat him as a thing to be ruled and not consulted. Let me at this stage make out a classificatory diagram of these elementary ideas of government in a modern country.

CLASS I.   It is supposed that the common man *can* govern :

> (1) without further organization (Anarchy) ;
> (2) through a majority vote by delegates.

CLASS II.   It is supposed that the common man *cannot* govern, and that government therefore must be through the agency of Able Persons who may be classified under one of the following sub-heads, either as

> (1) persons elected by the common man because he believes them to be persons able to govern—just as he chooses his doctors as persons able to secure health, and his electrical engineers as persons able to attend to his tramways, lighting, etc., etc. ;
> (2) persons of a special class, as, for example, persons born and educated to rule (e.g. *Aristocracy*), or rich business adventurers (*Plutocracy*) who rule without consulting the common man at all.
>
> To which two sub-classes we may perhaps add a sort of intermediate stage between them, namely :
> (3) persons elected by a special class of voter.

Monarchy may be either a special case of Class II. (1), (2) or (3), in which the persons who rule have narrowed down in number to one person, and the duration of monarchy may be either for life or a term of years. These two classes and the five sub-classes cover, I believe, all the elementary political types in our world.

Now in the constitution of a modern state, because of the conflict and confusion of ideas, all or most of these five sub-classes may usually be found intertwined. The British constitution, for instance, is a complicated tangle of arrangements, due to a struggle between the ideas of Class I. (2), Class II. (3), tending to become Class II. (1) and Class II. (2) in both its aristocratic and monarchist forms. The American constitution is largely dominated by Class I. (2), from which it breaks away in the case of the President to a short-term monarchist aspect of Class II. (1). I will not elaborate this classification further. I have made it here in order to render clear first, that what we moderns mean by democracy is not what the Greeks meant at all, that is to say, direct government by the assembly of all the citizens, and secondly and more important, that the word " democracy " is being used very largely in current discussion, so that it is impossible to say in any particular case whether the intention is Class I. (2) or Class II. (1), and that we have to make up our minds whether we mean, if I may coin two phrases, " delegate democracy " or " selective democracy," or some definite combination of these two, when we talk about " democracy," before we can get on much beyond a generous gesture of equality and enfranchisement towards our brother man.   The word is being used, in fact, confusingly for these two quite widely different things.

Now, it seems to me that though there has been no very clear discussion of the issue between those two very opposite conceptions of democracy, largely because of the want of proper distinctive terms, there has nevertheless been a wide movement of public opinion away from " delegate democracy " and towards " selective democracy."   People have gone on saying " democracy," while gradually changing its meaning from the former to the latter. It is notable in Great Britain, for example, that while there has been no perceptible diminution in our faith in democracy, there has been a growing criticism of " party " and " politicians," and a great weakening in the power and influence of representatives and representative institutions. There has been a growing demand for personality and initiative in elected persons.   The press, which was once entirely subordinate politically to parliamentary politics, adopts an attitude towards parliament and party leaders nowadays which would have seemed inconceivable insolence in the days of Lord Palmerston. And there has been a vigorous agitation in support of electoral methods which are manifestly calculated to subordinate " delegated " to " selected " men.

The movement for electoral reform in Great Britain at the present time is one of quite fundamental importance in the development of modern democracy. The case of the reformers is that heretofore modern democracy has not had a fair opportunity of showing its best possibilities to the world, because the methods of election have persistently set aside the better types of public men, or rather of would-be public men, in favour of mere party hacks. That is a story common to Britain and the American democracies, but in America it was expressed in rather different terms and dealt with in a less analytical fashion than it has been in Great Britain. It was not at first clearly understood that the failure of democracy to produce good government came through the preference of " delegated " over " selected " men, the idea of delegation did in fact dominate the minds of both electoral reformers and electoral conservatives alike, and the earlier stages of the reform movement in Great Britain were inspired not so much by the idea of getting a better type of

representative as by the idea of getting a fairer
representation of minorities. It was only slowly
that the idea that sensible men do not usually
belong to any political " party " took hold. It is
only now being realized that what sensible men
desire in a member of parliament is honour and
capacity rather than a mechanical loyalty to a
" platform." They do not want to dictate to their
representative ; they want a man they can trust
as their representative. In the fifties and sixties
of the last century, in which this electoral reform
movement began and the method of Proportional
Representation was thought out, it was possible
for the reformers to work untroubled upon the
assumption that if a man was not necessarily born a

> " . . . little Liber-al,
> or else a little Conservative,"

he must at least be a Liberal-Unionist or a Conservative Free-Trader. But seeking a fair representation for party minorities, these reformers
produced a system of voting at once simple and
incapable of manipulation, that leads straight, not
to the representation of small parties, but to a
type of democratic government by selected best
men.

Before giving the essential features of that
system, it may be well to state in its simplest form

the evils at which the reform aims. An election, the reformers point out, is not the simple matter it appears to be at the first blush. Methods of voting can be manipulated in various ways, and nearly every method has its own liability to falsification. We may take for illustration the commonest, simplest case—the case that is the perplexity of every clear-thinking voter under British or American conditions—the case of a constituency in which every elector has one vote, and which returns one representative to Parliament. The naïve theory on which people go is that all the possible candidates are put up, that each voter votes for the one he likes best, and that the best man wins. The bitter experience is that hardly ever are there more than two candidates, and still more rarely is either of these the best man possible. Suppose, for example, the constituency is mainly Conservative. A little group of pothouse politicians, wire-pullers, busybodies, local journalists, and small lawyers, working for various monetary interests, have " captured " the local Conservative organization. They have time and energy to capture it, because they have no other interest in life except that. It is their " business," and honest men are busy with other duties. For reasons that do not appear these local " workers " put up an unknown Mr. Goldbug as the official Conservative

candidate. He professes a generally Conservative
view of things, but few people are sure of him and
few people trust him. Against him the weaker
(and therefore still more venal) Liberal organization
now puts up a Mr. Kentshire (formerly Wurstberg)
to represent the broader thought and finer generosi-
ties of the English mind. A number of Conservative
gentlemen, generally too busy about their honest
businesses to attend the party " smokers " and
the party cave, realize suddenly that they want
Goldbug hardly more than they want Wurstberg.
They put up their long-admired, trusted, and
able friend Mr. Sanity as an Independent Conservative.

Every one knows the trouble that follows. Mr.
Sanity is " going to split the party vote." The
hesitating voter is told, with considerable truth,
that a vote given for Mr. Sanity is a vote given for
Wurstberg. At any price the constituency does
not want Wurstberg. So at the eleventh hour
Mr. Sanity is induced to withdraw, and Mr. Goldbug goes into Parliament to misrepresent this
constituency. And so with most constituencies,
and the result is a legislative body consisting
largely of men of unknown character and obscure
aims, whose only credential is the wearing of a
party label. They come into parliament not to
forward the great interests they ostensibly support,

but with an eye to the railway jobbery, corporation business, concessions and financial operations that necessarily go on in and about the national legislature. That in its simplest form is the dilemma of democracy. The problem that has confronted modern democracy since its beginning has not really been the representation of organized minorities—they are very well able to look after themselves—but *the protection of the unorganized mass of busily occupied, fairly intelligent men from the tricks of the specialists who work the party machines.* We know Mr. Sanity, we want Mr. Sanity, but we are too busy to watch the incessant intrigues to oust him in favour of the obscurely influential people, politically docile, who are favoured by the organization. We want an organizer-proof method of voting. It is in answer to this demand, as the outcome of a most careful examination of the ways in which voting may be protected from the exploitation of those who *work* elections, that the method of Proportional Representation with a single transferable vote has been evolved. It is organizer-proof. It defies the caucus. If you do not like Mr. Goldbug you can put up and vote for Mr. Sanity, giving Mr. Goldbug your second choice, in the most perfect confidence that in any case your vote cannot help to return Mr. Wurstberg.

With Proportional Representation with a single transferable vote (this specification is necessary, because there are also the inferior imitations of various election-riggers figuring as proportional representation), it is *impossible to prevent the effective candidature of independent men of repute beside the official candidates.*

The method of voting under the Proportional Representation system has been ignorantly represented as complex. It is really almost ideally simple. You mark the list of candidates with numbers in the order of your preference. For example, you believe A to be absolutely the best man for parliament; you mark him 1. But B you think is the next best man; you mark him 2. That means that if A gets an enormous amount of support, ever so many more votes than he requires for his return, your vote will not be wasted. Only so much of your vote as is needed will go to A; the rest will go to B. Or, on the other hand, if A has so little support that his chances are hopeless, you will not have thrown your vote away upon him; it will go to B. Similarly you may indicate a third, a fourth, and a fifth choice; if you like you may mark every name on your paper with a number to indicate the order of your preferences. And that is all the voter has to do. The reckoning and counting of the votes presents not the slightest difficulty to any one used to the business of computation. Silly and dishonest men, appealing to still sillier audiences, have got themselves and their audiences into humorous muddles over this business, but the principles are perfectly plain and simple. Let me state them here; they can be fully and exactly stated, with various ornaments, comments, arguments, sarcastic remarks, and digressions, in seventy lines of this type.

It will be evident that, in any election under this system, any one who has got a certain proportion of No. 1 votes will be elected. If, for instance, five people have to be elected and 20,000 voters vote, then any one who has got 4001 first votes or more *must* be elected. 4001 votes is in that case enough to elect a candidate. This sufficient number of votes is called the *quota*, and any one who has more than that number of votes has obviously got more votes than is needful for election. So, to begin with, the voting papers are classified according to their first votes, and any candidates who have got more than a quota of first votes are forthwith declared elected. But most of these elected men would under the old system waste votes because they would have too many; for manifestly a candidate who gets more than the quota of votes *needs only a fraction of each of these votes to return him.* If, for instance, he gets double

the quota he needs only half each vote. He takes
that fraction, therefore, under this new and better
system, and the rest of each vote is entered on to
No. 2 upon that voting paper. And so on. Now
this is an extremely easy job for an accountant
or skilled computer, and it is quite easily checked
by any other accountant and skilled computer.
A reader with a bad arithmetical education,
ignorant of the very existence of such a thing as
a slide rule, knowing nothing of account keeping,
who thinks of himself working out the resultant
fractions with a stumpy pencil on a bit of greasy
paper in a bad light, may easily think of this transfer
of fractions as a dangerous and terrifying process.
It is, for a properly trained man, the easiest, exact-
est job conceivable. The Cash Register people will
invent machines to do it for you while you wait.
What happens, then, is that every candidate with
more than a quota, beginning with the top candidate, sheds a fraction of each vote he has received,
down the list, and the next one sheds his surplus
fraction in the same way, and so on until candidates
lower in the list, who are at first below the quota,
fill up to it. When all the surplus votes of the
candidates at the head of the list have been disposed of, then the hopeless candidates at the bottom
of the list are dealt with. The second votes on
their voting papers are treated as whole votes and

distributed up the list, and so on. It will be plain
to the quick-minded that, towards the end, there
will be a certain chasing about of little fractions
of votes, and a slight modification of the quota
due to voting papers having no second or third
preferences marked upon them, a chasing about
that it will be difficult for an untrained intelligence to follow. *But untrained intelligences are
not required to follow it.* For the skilled computer
these things offer no difficulty at all. And they
are not difficulties of principle but of manipulation.
One might as well refuse to travel in a taxicab
until the driver had explained the magneto as
refuse to accept the principle of Proportional
Representation by the single transferable vote
until one had remedied all the deficiencies of one's
arithmetical education. The fundamental principle
of the thing, that a candidate who gets more votes
than he wants is made to hand on a fraction of
each vote to the voter's second choice, and that
a candidate whose chances are hopeless is made
to hand on the whole vote to the voter's second
choice, so that practically only a small number
of votes are ineffective, is within the compass of
the mind of a boy of ten.

But simple as this method is, it completely kills
the organization and manipulation of voting. It
completely solves the Goldbug-Wurstberg-Sanity

problem. It is knave-proof—short of forging, stealing, or destroying voting papers. A man of repute, a leaderly man, may defy all the party organizations in existence and stand beside and be returned over the head of a worthless man, though the latter be smothered with party labels. That is the gist of this business. The difference in effect between Proportional Representation and the old method of voting must ultimately be to change the moral and intellectual quality of elected persons profoundly. People are only beginning to realize the huge possibilities of advance inherent in this change of political method. It means no less than a revolution from " delegate democracy " to " selective democracy."

Now, I will not pretend to be anything but a strong partizan in this matter. When I speak of " democracy " I mean " selective democracy." I believe that " delegate democracy " is already provably a failure in the world, and that the reason why to-day, after three and a half years of struggle, we are still fighting German autocracy and fighting with no certainty of absolute victory, is because the affairs of the three great Atlantic democracies have been largely in the hands not of selected men but of delegated men, men of intrigue and the party machine, of dodges rather than initiatives, second-rate men. When Lord Haldane, defending his

K

party for certain insufficiencies in their preparation
for the eventuality of the great war, pleaded that
they had no " mandate " from the country to do
anything of the sort, he did more than commit
political suicide, he bore conclusive witness against
the whole system which had made him what he
was. Neither Britain nor France in this struggle
has produced better statesmen nor better generals
than the German autocracy. The British and
French Foreign Offices are old monarchist organizations still. To this day the British and French
politicians haggle and argue with the German
ministers upon petty points and debating society
advantages, smart and cunning, while the peoples
perish. The one man who has risen to the greatness
of this great occasion, the man who is, in default
of any rival, rapidly becoming the leader of the
world towards peace, is neither a delegate politician nor the choice of a monarch and his council-
lors. He is the one authoritative figure in these
transactions whose mind has not been subdued
either by long discipline in the party machine or
by court intrigue, who has continued his education
beyond those early twenties when the mind of the
" budding politician " ceases to expand, who has
thought, and thought things out, who is an educated
man among dexterous under-educated specialists.
By something very like a belated accident in the

framing of the American constitution, the President of the United States is more in the nature of a selected man than any other conspicuous figure at the present time. He is specially elected by a special electoral college after an elaborate preliminary selection of candidates by the two great party machines. And be it remembered that Mr. Wilson is not the first great President the United States have had, he is one of a series of figures who tower over their European contemporaries. The United States have had many advantageous circumstances to thank for their present ascendancy in the world's affairs : isolation from militarist pressure for a century and a quarter, a vast virgin continent, plenty of land, freedom from centralization, freedom from titles and social vulgarities, common schools, a real democratic spirit in its people, and a great enthusiasm for universities ; but no single advantage has been so great as this happy accident which has given it a specially selected man as its voice and figurehead in the world's affairs. In the average congressman, in the average senator, as Ostrogorski's great book so industriously demonstrated, the United States have no great occasion for pride. Neither the Senate nor the House of Representatives seem to rise above the level of the British Houses of Parliament, with a Government unable to control the rebel forces of Ulster, unable to promote or dismiss generals without an outcry, weakly amenable to the press, and terrifyingly incapable of great designs. It is to the United States of America we must look now if the world is to be made " safe for democracy." It is to the method of selection, as distinguished from delegation, that we must look if democracy is to be saved from itself.

X

THE RECENT STRUGGLE FOR PROPORTIONAL REPRESENTATION IN GREAT BRITAIN

BRITISH political life resists cleansing with all the vigour of a dirty little boy. It is nothing to your politician that the economic and social organization of all the world is strained almost to the pitch of collapse, and that it is vitally important to mankind that everywhere the whole will and intelligence of the race should be enlisted in the great tasks of making a permanent peace and reconstructing the shattered framework of society. These are remote, unreal considerations to the politician. What is the world to him? He has scarcely heard of it. He has been far too busy as a politician. He has been thinking of smart little tricks in the lobby and brilliant exploits at question time. He has been thinking of jobs and appointments, of whether Mr. Asquith is likely to " come back " and how far it is safe to bank upon L. G. His one supreme purpose is to keep affairs in the hands of his own specialized set, to keep the old obscure party game going, to rig his little tricks behind a vast, silly camouflage of sham issues, to keep out able men and disinterested men, the public mind, and the general intelligence, from any effective interference with his disastrous manipulations of the common weal.

I do not see how any intelligent and informed man can have followed the recent debates in the House of Commons upon Proportional Representation without some gusts of angry contempt. They were the most pitiful and alarming demonstration of the intellectual and moral quality of British public life at the present time.

From the wire-pullers of the Fabian Society and from the party organizers of both Liberal and Tory party alike, and from the knowing cards, the pot-house shepherds, and jobbing lawyers who " work " the constituencies, comes the chief opposition to this straightening out of our electoral system so urgently necessary and so long overdue. They have fought it with a zeal and efficiency that is rarely displayed in the nation's interest. From nearly every outstanding man outside that little inner world of political shams and dodges, who has given any attention to the question, comes, on the other hand, support for this reform. Even the great party leaders, Mr. Balfour and Mr. Asquith, were in its favour. One might safely judge this question by considering who are the advocates on either side. But the best arguments for Proportional Representation arise out of its opponents' speeches, and to these I will confine my attention now. Consider Lord Harcourt—heir to the most sacred traditions of the party game—hurling scorn at a project that would introduce "faddists, mugwumps," and so on and so on—in fact independent thinking men—into the legislature. Consider the value of Lord Curzon's statement that London "rose in revolt" against the project. Do you remember that day, dear reader, when the streets of London boiled with passionate men shouting, "No Proportional Representation! Down with Proportional Representation"? You don't. Nor do I. But what happened was that the guinea-pigs and solicitors and nobodies, the party hacks who form the bulk of London's misrepresentation in the House of Commons, stampeded in terror against a proposal that threatened to wipe them out and replace them by known and responsible men. London, alas! does not seem to care how its members are elected. What Londoner knows anything about his member? Hundreds of thousands of Londoners do not even know which of the ridiculous constituencies into which the politicians have dismembered our London they are in. Only as I was writing this in my flat in St. James's Court, Westminster, did it occur to me to inquire who was representing me in the councils of the nation while I write. . . .

After some slight difficulty I ascertained that my representative is a Mr. Burdett Coutts, who was, in the romantic eighties, Mr. Ashmead-Bartlett. And by a convenient accident I find that the other day he moved to reject the Proportional Representation Amendment made by the House of Lords to the Representation of the People Bill, so that I am able to look up the debate in Hansard and study my opinions as he represented them and this question at one and the same time. And, taking little things first, I am proud and happy to discover that the member for me was the only participator in the debate who, in the vulgar and reprehensible phrase, " threw a dead cat," or, in polite terms, displayed classical learning. My member said, " *Timeo Danaos et dona ferentes*," with a rather graceful compliment to the Labour Conference at Nottingham. " I could not help thinking to myself," said my member, " that at that conference there must have been many men of sufficient classical reading to say to themselves, ' *Timeo Danaos et dona ferentes*.' " In which surmise he was quite right. Except perhaps for " *Tempus fugit*," " *verbum sap.*," " *Arma virumque*," and " *Quis custodiet*," there is no better known relic of antiquity. But my member went a little beyond

my ideas when he said : " We are asked to enter
upon a method of legislation which can bear no
other description than that of law-making in the
dark," because I think it can bear quite a lot of
other descriptions. This was, however, the artistic
prelude to a large, vague, gloomy dissertation about
nothing very definite, a muddling up of the main
question with the minor issue of a schedule of
constituencies involved in the proposal.

The other parts of my member's speech do not,
I confess, fill me with the easy confidence I would
like to feel in my proxy. Let me extract a few
gems of eloquence from the speech of this voice
which speaks for me, and give also the only argument he advanced that needs consideration. " History repeats itself," he said, " very often in curious
ways as to facts, but generally with very different
results." That, honestly, I like. It is a sentence
one can read over several times. But he went on
to talk of the entirely different scheme for minority
representation, which was introduced into the
Reform Bill of 1867, and there I am obliged to
part company with him. That was a silly scheme
for giving two votes to each voter in a three-
member constituency. It has about as much
resemblance to the method of scientific voting
under discussion as a bath-chair has to an aeroplane.
" But that measure of minority representation

led to a baneful invention," my representative went on to say, " and left behind it a hateful memory in the Birmingham caucus. I well remember that when I stood for Parliament thirty-two years ago *we had no better platform weapon than repeating over and over again in a sentence the name of Mr. Schnadhorst,* and I am not sure that it would not serve the same purpose now. Under that system the work of the caucus was, of course, far simpler than it will be if this system ever comes into operation. All the caucus had to do under that measure was to divide the electors into three groups and with three candidates, A., B., and C., to order one group to vote for A. and B., another for B. and C., and the third for A. and C., and they carried the whole of their candidates and kept them for many years. But the multiplicity of ordinal preferences, second, third, fourth, fifth, up to tenth, which the single transferable vote system would involve, will require a more scientific handling in party interests, and neither party will be able to face an election with any hope of success without the assistance of the most drastic form of caucus and *without its orders being carried out by the electors.*"

Now, I swear by Heaven that, lowly creature as I am, a lost vote, a nothing, voiceless and helpless in public affairs, I am not going to stand the imputation that that sort of reasoning represents the average mental quality of Westminster—outside Parliament, that is. Most of my neighbours in St. James's Court, for example, have quite large pieces of head above their eyebrows. Read these above sentences over and ponder their significance —so far as they have any significance. Never mind my keen personal humiliation at this display of the mental calibre of my representative, but consider what the mental calibre of a House must be that did not break out into loud guffaws at such a passage. The line of argument is about as lucid as if one reasoned that because one can break a window with a stone it is no use buying a telescope. And it remains entirely a matter for speculation whether my member is arguing that a caucus *can* rig an election carried on under the Proportional Representation system or that it cannot. At the first blush it seems to read as if he intended the former. But be careful ! Did he ? Let me suggest that in that last sentence he really expresses the opinion that it cannot. It can be read either way. Electors under modern conditions are not going to obey the " orders " of even the " most drastic caucus "—whatever a " drastic caucus " may be. Why should they ? In the Birmingham instance it was only a section of the majority, voting by wards, in an election on purely party lines, which " obeyed " in order to keep out the minority party candidate. I think myself that my member's mind waggled. Perhaps his real thoughts shone out through an argument not intended to betray them. What he did say as much as he said anything was that under Proportional Representation, elections are going to be very troublesome and difficult for party candidates. If that was his intention, then, after all, I forgive him much. I think that and more than that. I think that they are going to make party candidates who are merely party candidates impossible. That is exactly what we reformers are after. Then I shall get a representative more to my taste than Mr. Burdett Coutts.

But let me turn now to the views of other people's representatives.

Perhaps the most damning thing ever said against the present system, damning because of its empty absurdity, was uttered by Sir Thomas Whittaker. He was making the usual exaggerations of the supposed difficulties of the method. He said English people didn't like such " complications." They like a " straight fight between two men." Think of it ! A straight fight ! For more than a quarter-century I have been a voter, usually with votes in two or three constituencies, and never in all that long political life have I seen a single straight fight in an election, but only the dismallest sham fights it is possible to conceive. Thrice only in all that time have I cast a vote for a man whom I respected. On all other occasions the election that mocked my citizenship was either an arranged walk-over for one party or the other, or I had a choice between two unknown persons, mysteriously selected as candidates by obscure busy people with local interests in the constituency. Every intelligent person knows that this is the usual experience of a free and independent voter in England. The " fight " of an ordinary Parliamentary election in England is about as " straight " as the business of a thimble rigger.

And consider just what these " complications " are of which the opponents of Proportional Representation chant so loudly. In the sham election of to-day, which the politicians claim gives them a mandate to muddle up our affairs, the voter puts a × against the name of the least detestable of the two candidates that are thrust upon him. Under the Proportional Representation method there will be a larger constituency, a larger list of candidates, and a larger number of people to be elected, and he will put 1 against the name of the man he most wants to be elected, 2 against his second choice, and if he likes he may indulge in marking a third, or even a further choice. He may, if he thinks fit, number off the whole list of candidates. That is all he will have to do. That is the stupendous intricacy of the method that flattens out the minds of Lord Harcourt and Sir Thomas Whittaker. And as for the working of it, if you must go into that, all that happens is that if your first choice gets more votes than he needs for his return, he takes only the fraction of your vote that he requires, and the rest of the vote goes on to your Number 2. If 2 isn't in need of all of it, the rest goes on to 3. And so on. That is the profound mathematical mystery, that is the riddle beyond the wit of Westminster, which overpowers these fine intelligences and sets them babbling of " senior wranglers." Each time there is a debate on this question in the House, member after member hostile to the proposal will play the ignorant fool and pretend to be confused himself, and will try to confuse others, by deliberately clumsy statements of these most elementary ideas. Surely if there were no other argument for a change of type in the House, these poor knitted brows, these public perspirations of the gentry who " cannot understand P.R.," should suffice.

But let us be just ; it is not all pretence ; the inability of Mr. Austen Chamberlain to grasp the simple facts before him was undoubtedly genuine. He followed Mr. Burdett Coutts, in support of Mr. Burdett Coutts, with the most Christian disregard of the nasty things Mr. Burdett Coutts had seemed to be saying about the Birmingham caucus from which he sprang. He had a childish story to tell of how voters would not give their first votes to their real preferences, because they would assume he "would get in in any case"—God knows why. Of course on the assumption that the voter behaves like an idiot, anything is possible. And never apparently having heard of fractions, this great Birmingham leader was unable to understand that a voter who puts 1 against a candidate's name votes for that candidate anyhow. He could not imagine any feeling on the part of the voter that No. 1 was his man. A vote is a vote to this simple rather than lucid mind, a thing one and indivisible. Read this—

"Birmingham," he said, referring to a Schedule under consideration, "is to be cut into three constituencies of four members each. I am to have a constituency of 100,000 electors, I suppose. How many thousand inhabitants I do not know. *Every effort will be made to prevent any of those electors knowing—in fact, it would be impossible for any of them to know—whether they voted for me or not, or at any rate whether they effectively voted for me or not, or whether the vote which they wished to give to me was really diverted to somebody else.*"

Only in a house of habitually inattentive men could any one talk such nonsense without reproof, but I look in vain through Hansard's record of this debate for a single contemptuous reference to Mr. Chamberlain's obtuseness. And the rest of his speech was a lamentable account of the time and trouble he would have to spend upon his constituents if the new method came in. He was the perfect figure of the parochially important person in a state of defensive excitement. No doubt his speech appealed to many in the House.

Of course Lord Harcourt was quite right in saying that the character of the average House of Commons member will be changed by Proportional Representation. It will. It will make the election of obscure and unknown men, of carpet-bag candidates who work a constituency as a hawker works a village, of local pomposities and village-pump " leaders " almost impossible. It will replace such candidates by better known and more widely known men. It will make the House of Commons so much the more a real gathering of the nation, so much the more a house of representative men. (Lord Harcourt's " faddists and mugwumps.") And it is perfectly true as Mr. Ramsay Macdonald (also an opponent) declares, that Proportional Representation means constituencies so big that it will be impossible for a poor man to cultivate and work them. That is unquestionable. But, mark another point, it will also make it useless, as Mr. Chamberlain has testified, for rich men to cultivate and work them. All this cultivating and working, all this going about and making things right with this little jobber here, that contractor there, all the squaring of small political clubs and organizations, all the subscription black-mail and charity bribery, that now makes a Parliamentary candidature so utterly rotten an influence upon public life, will be killed dead by Proportional Representation. You cannot job men into Parliament by Proportional Representa-tion. Proportional Representation lets in the outsider. It lets in the common, unassigned voter who isn't in the local clique. That is the clue to nearly all this opposition of the politicians. It makes democracy possible for the first time in modern history. And that poor man of Mr. Ramsay Macdonald's imagination, instead of cadging about a constituency in order to start politician, will have to make good in some more useful way—as a leader of the workers in their practical affairs, for example —before people will hear of him and begin to believe in him.

The opposition to Proportional Representation of Mr. Sidney Webb and his little circle is a trifle more " scientific " in tone than these naïve objec-tions of the common run of antagonist, but under-lying it is the same passionate desire to keep politics a close game for the politician and to bar out the politically unspecialized man. There is more conceit and less jobbery behind the criticisms of this type of mind. It is an opposition based on the idea that the common man is a fool who does not know what is good for him. So he has to be stampeded. Politics, according to this school, is a sort of cattle-driving.

The Webbites do not deny the broad facts of the case. Our present electoral system, with our big modern constituencies of thousands of voters, leads to huge turnovers of political power with a relatively small shifting of public opinion. It makes a mock of public opinion by caricature, and Parliament becomes the distorting mirror of the nation. Under some loud false issue a few score of thousands of votes turn over, and in goes this party or that with a big sham majority. This the Webbites admit. But they applaud it. It gives us, they say, "a strong Government." Public opinion, the intelligent man outside the House, is ruled out of the game. He has no power of intervention at all. The artful little Fabian politicians rub their hands and say, " *Now* we can get to work with the wires ! No one can stop us." And when the public complains of the results, there is always the repartee, " *You* elected them." But the Fabian psychology is the psychology of a very small group of pedants who believe that fair ends may be reached by foul means. It is much easier and more natural to serve foul ends by foul means. In practice it is not tricky benevolence but tricky bargaining among the interests that will secure control of the political wires. That is a bad enough state of affairs in ordinary times, but in times of tragic necessity like the present men will not be mocked in this way. Life is going to be very intense in the years ahead of us. If we go right on to another caricature Parliament, with perhaps half a hundred leading men in it and the rest hacks and nobodies, the baffled and discontented outsiders in the streets may presently be driven to rioting and the throwing of bombs. Unless, indeed, the insurrection of the outsiders takes a still graver form, and the Press, which has ceased entirely to be a Party Press in Great Britain, helps some adventurous Prime Minister to flout and set aside the lower House altogether. There is neither much moral nor much physical force behind the House of Commons at the present time.

The argument of the Fabian opponents to Proportional Representation is frankly that the strongest Government is got in a House of half a hundred or fewer leading men, with the rest of the Parliament driven sheep. But the whole mischief of the present system is that the obscure members of Parliament are not sheep; they are a crowd of little-minded, second-rate men just as greedy and eager and self-seeking as any of us. They vote straight indeed on all the main party questions, they obey their Whips like sheep then; but there is a great bulk of business in Parliament outside the main party questions, and obedience is not without its price. These are matters vitally affecting our railways and ships and communications generally, the food and health of the people, armaments, every sort of employment, the appointment of public servants, the everyday texture of all our lives. Then the nobody becomes somebody, the party hack gets busy, the rat is in the granary. . . .

In these recent debates in the House of Commons one can see every stock trick of the wire-puller in operation. Particularly we have the old dodge of the man who is " in theory quite in sympathy with Proportional Representation, but . . ." It is, he declares regretfully, too late. It will cause delay. Difficult to make arrangements. Later on perhaps. And so on. It is never too late for a vital issue. Upon the speedy adoption of Proportional Representation depends, as Mr. Balfour made plain in an admirable speech, whether the great occasions of the peace and after the peace are to be handled by a grand council of all that is best and most leaderlike in the nation, or whether they are to be left to a few leaders, apparently leading, but really profoundly swayed by the obscure crowd of politicians and jobbers behind them. Are the politicians to hamper and stifle us in this supreme crisis of our national destinies or are we British peoples to have a real control of our own affairs in this momentous time ? Are men of light and purpose to have a voice in public affairs or not ? Proportional Representation is supremely a test question. It is a question that no adverse decision in the House of Commons can stifle. There are too many people now who grasp its importance and significance. Every one who sets a proper value upon purity in public life and the vitality of democratic institutions will, I am convinced, vote and continue to vote across every other question against the antiquated, foul, and fraudulent electoral methods that have hitherto robbed democracy of three-quarters of its efficiency.

XI

THE STUDY AND PROPAGANDA OF DEMOCRACY

IN the preceding chapter I have dealt with the discussion of Proportional Representation in the British House of Commons in order to illustrate the intellectual squalor amidst which public affairs have to be handled at the present time, even in a country professedly " democratic." I have taken this one discussion as a sample to illustrate the present imperfection of our democratic instrument. All over the world, in every country, great multitudes of intelligent and serious people are now inspired by the idea of a new order of things in the world, of a world-wide establishment of peace and mutual aid between nation and nation and man and man. But, chiefly because of the elementary crudity of existing electoral methods, hardly anywhere at present, except at Washington, do these great ideas and this world-wide will find expression. Amidst the other politicians and statesmen of the world President Wilson towers up with an effect almost divine.

But it is no ingratitude to him to say that he is not nearly so exceptional a being among educated men as he is among the official leaders of mankind. Everywhere now one may find something of the Wilson purpose and intelligence, but nearly everywhere it is silenced or muffled or made ineffective by the political advantage of privileged or of violent and adventurous inferior men. He is " one of us," but it is his good fortune to have got his head out of the sack that is about the heads of most of us. In the official world, in the world of rulers and representatives and " statesmen," he almost alone, speaks for the modern intelligence.

This general stifling of the better intelligence of the world and its possible release to expression and power, seems to me to be the fundamental issue underlying all the present troubles of mankind. We cannot get on while everywhere fools and vulgarians hold the levers that can kill, imprison, silence and starve men. We cannot get on with false government and we cannot get on with mob government; we must have right government. The intellectual people of the world have a duty of co-operation they have too long neglected. The modernization of political institutions, the study of these institutions until we have worked out and achieved the very best and most efficient methods whereby the whole community of mankind may work together under the direction of its chosen intelligences, is the common duty of every one who has a brain for the service. And before everything else we have to realize this crudity and imperfection in what we call " democracy " at the present time. Democracy is still chiefly an aspiration, it is a spirit, it is an idea ; for the most part its methods are still to seek. And still more is this " League of Free Nations " as yet but an aspiration. Let us not underrate the task before us. Only the disinterested devotion of hundreds of thousands of active brains in school, in pulpit, in book and press and assembly can ever bring these redeeming conceptions down to the solid earth to rule.

All round the world there is this same obscuration of the real intelligence of men. In Germany, human good will and every fine mind are subordinated to political forms that have for a mouthpiece a Chancellor with his brains manifestly addled by the theories of *Welt-Politik* and the Bismarckian tradition, and for a figurehead a mad Kaiser. Nevertheless there comes even from Germany muffled cries for a new age. A grinning figure like a bloodstained Punch is all that speaks for the best brains in Bulgaria. Yes. We Western allies know all that by heart ; but, after all, the immediate question for each one of us is, " *What*

speaks for me? " So far as official political forms
go I myself am as ineffective as any right-thinking
German or Bulgarian could possibly be. I am more
ineffective than a Galician Pole or a Bohemian
who votes for his nationalist representative.
Politically I am a negligible item in the constituency of this Mr. Burdett Coutts into whose
brain we have been peeping. Politically I am
less than a waistcoat button on that quaint figure.
And that is all I am—except that I revolt. I have
written of it so far as if it were just a joke. But
indeed bad and foolish political institutions cannot
be a joke. Sooner or later they prove themselves
to be tragedy. This war is that. It is yesterday's
lazy, tolerant, "sense of humour" wading out now
into the lakes of blood it refused to foresee.

It is absurd to suppose that anywhere to-day
the nationalisms, the suspicions and hatreds, the
cants and policies, and dead phrases that sway
men represent the current intelligence of mankind.
They are merely the evidences of its disorganiza-
tion. Even now we *know* we could do far better.
Give mankind but a generation or so of peace and
right education and this world could mock at the
poor imaginations that conceived a millennium.
But we have to get intelligences together, we have
to canalize thought before it can work and produce
its due effects. To that end, I suppose, there has

been a vast amount of mental activity among us political "negligibles." For my own part I have thought of the idea of God as the banner of human unity and justice, and I have made some tentatives in that direction, but men, I perceive, have argued themselves mean and petty about religion. At the word " God " passions bristle. The word " God " does not unite men, it angers them. But I doubt if God cares greatly whether we call Him God or no. His service is the service of man. This double idea of the League of Free Nations, linked with the idea of democracy as universal justice, is free from the jealousy of the theologians and great enough for men to unite upon everywhere. I know how warily one must reckon with the spite of the priest, but surely these ideas may call upon the teachers of all the great world religions for their support. The world is full now of confused propaganda, propaganda of national ideas, of traditions of hate, of sentimental and degrading loyalties, of every sort of error that divides and tortures and slays mankind. All human institutions are made of propaganda, are sustained by propaganda and perish when it ceases; they must be continually explained and re-explained to the young and the negligent. And for this new world of democracy and the League of Free Nations to which all reasonable men are looking, there must needs be the greatest of all propagandas. For that cause every one must become a teacher and a missionary. " Persuade to it and make the idea of it and the necessity for it plain," that is the duty of every school teacher, every tutor, every religious teacher, every writer, every lecturer, every parent, every trusted friend throughout the world. For it, too, every one must become a student, must go on with the task of making vague intentions into definite intentions, of analyzing and destroying obstacles, of mastering the ten thousand difficulties of detail. . . .

I am a man who looks now towards the end of life ; fifty-one years have I scratched off from my calendar, another slips by, and I cannot tell how many more of the sparse remainder of possible years are really mine. I live in days of hardship and privation, when it seems more natural to feel ill than well ; without holidays or rest or peace ; friends and the sons of my friends have been killed; death seems to be feeling always now for those I most love; the newspapers that come in to my house tell mostly of blood and disaster, of drownings and slaughterings, of cruelties and base intrigues. Yet never have I been so sure that there is a divinity in man and that a great order of human life, a reign of justice and world-wide happiness, of plenty, power, hope, and gigantic creative effort, lies close at hand. Even now we have the science and the ability available for a universal welfare, though it is scattered about the world like a handful of money dropped by a child; even now there exists all the knowledge that is needed to make mankind universally free and human life sweet and noble. We need but the faith for it, and it is at hand; we need but the courage to lay our hands upon it and in a little space of years it can be ours.

THE END

PRINTED IN ENGLAND BY
WILLIAM CLOWES AND SONS, LIMITED, LONDON AND BECCLES.

ALPHABETICAL CATALOGUE OF BOOKS
IN
GENERAL LITERATURE AND FICTION

PUBLISHED BY

PERCY SPALDING,
ANDREW CHATTO,
C. H. C. PRENTICE,
C. F. M. TOZER.

CHATTO & WINDUS

97 & 99 ST. MARTIN'S LANE, CHARING CROSS

Telegrams
Bookstore, London

LONDON, W.C. 2

Telephone No.
1624 Gerrard

ADAM (GEORGE).—Behind the Scenes at the Front. With a Frontispiece. Demy 8vo, cloth, 6s. net.

ADAMS (W. DAVENPORT).— A Dictionary of the Drama. Vol. I. (A to G). Demy 8vo, cl., 10s. 6d. net.

ALLEN (GRANT), Books by.
Crown 8vo, cloth, 3s. 6d. net each.
Babylon. With 12 Illustrations.
Strange Stories.
The Beckoning Hand.
For Maimie's Sake.
Philistia.
The Devil's Die.
In all Shades.
Tents of Shem.
This Mortal Coil.
Dumaresq's Daughter.
Under Sealed Orders.
The Duchess of Powysland.
Blood Royal. | The Great Taboo.
Ivan Greet's Masterpiece.
The Scallywag. With 24 Illustrations.
At Market Value.

The Tents of Shem. POPULAR EDITION, medium 8vo, 9d. net.

ALEXANDER (Mrs.), Novels by.
Crown 8vo, cloth, 3s. 6d. net each.
Valerie's Fate. | Mona's Choice.
A Life Interest. | Blind Fate.
By Woman's Wit.
The Cost of her Pride.
A Golden Autumn.
Barbara, Lady's Maid & Peeress.
Mrs. Crichton's Creditor.
A Missing Hero.
A Fight with Fate.
The Step-mother.

ANTROBUS (C. L.), Novels by.
Crown 8vo, cloth, 3s. 6d. net each.
Quality Corner. | Wildersmoor.
The Wine of Finvarra.
The Stone Ezel.

ARCHER (WILLIAM). The Pirate's Progress. Demy 8vo. Coloured wrapper, 3d. net.

ART : A Critical Essay. By CLIVE BELL. With 6 Illustrations. Crown 8vo, buckram, 5s. net.

ARNOLD (E. L.), Stories by.
The Wonderful Adventures of Phra the Phœnician. Crown 8vo, cloth, with 12 Illusts. by H. M. PAGET, 3s. 6d. net.

The Constable of St. Nicholas. With a Frontispiece. Crown 8vo, cloth, 3s. 6d. net.

ART and LETTERS LIBRARY (The) Large crown 8vo. Each volume with 8 Coloured Plates, and 24 in Halftone. Bound in cloth, 5s. net per vol. EDITION DE LUXE, small 4to, printed on pure rag paper, with additional Plates, parchment, 10s. 6d. net per vol.

Stories of the Italian Artists from Vasari. Collected and arranged by E. L. SEELEY.

Artists of the Italian Renaissance: their Stories as set forth by Vasari, Ridolfi, Lanzi, and the Chroniclers. Collected and arranged by E. L. SEELEY.

Stories of the Flemish and Dutch Artists, from the Time of the Van Eycks to the End of the Seventeenth Century, drawn from Contemporary Records. Collected and arranged by VICTOR REYNOLDS.

Stories of the English Artists, from Van Dyck to Turner (1600-1851). Collected and arranged by RANDALL DAVIES and CECIL HUNT.

Stories of the French Artists, from Clouet to Delacroix. Collected and arranged by P. M. TURNER and C. H. COLLINS BAKER.

Stories of the Spanish Artists until Goya. By SIR WILLIAM STIRLING-MAXWELL. Selected and arranged by LUIS CARREÑO. With Introduction by EDWARD HUTTON.

Stories of the German Artists. By Prof. Dr. HANS W. SINGER.

The Little Flowers of S. Francis of Assisi. Translated by Prof. T. W. ARNOLD. With 8 Illustrations in Colour and 24 in Half-tone.

ART & LETTERS LIBRARY—contd.

Of the Imitation of Christ. By THOMAS À KEMPIS. Translated by RICHARD WHYTFORD. With Historical Introduction by WILFRID RAYNAL, O.S.B., and 8 Reproductions in Colour and other decorations by W. RUSSELL FLINT. The EDITION DE LUXE has four additional Plates in Colour and may be had bound in pigskin with clasps, 25s. net.

The Confessions of Saint Augustine Translated by Dr. E. B. PUSEY. Edited by TEMPLE SCOTT. With an Introduction by Mrs. MEYNELL, and 12 Plates in Colour by MAXWELL ARMFIELD. The EDITION DE LUXE may be had bound in pigskin with clasps. 25s. net.

The Master of Game: The Oldest English Book on Hunting. By EDWARD, Second Duke of York. Edited by W. A. and F. BAILLIE-GROHMAN. Introduction by THEODORE ROOSEVELT, Photogravure Frontispiece and 23 full-page Illustrations. Large crown 8vo, cloth, 7s. 6d. net; parchment, 10s. 6d. net.

ARTEMUS WARD'S Works.
Crown 8vo, cloth, with Portrait, 3s. 6d. net.

ARTIST (The Mind of the).
Edited by Mrs. LAURENCE BINYON. With 8 Plates. Small cr. 8vo, cloth, 3s. 6d. net.

ASHTON (JOHN).—Social Life in the Reign of Queen Anne.
With 85 Illusts. Crown 8vo, cloth, 3s. 6d. net.

ATKINS (J. B.) and CYRIL IONIDES.—A Floating Home.
The Log of a Thames Sailing Barge. With 8 Coloured Illustrations by Arnold Bennett. Fcap. 4to, cloth, 10s. 6d. net.

AUSTEN (JANE), The Works of,
in Ten Volumes, each containing Ten Illustrations in Colour by A. WALLIS MILLS. With Notes by R. BRIMLEY JOHNSON. Post 8vo, cloth, 3s. 6d. net per vol. The Novels are as follows : I. and II., PRIDE AND PREJUDICE; III. and IV., SENSE AND SENSIBILITY; V., NORTHANGER ABBEY; VI., PERSUASION; VII. and VIII. EMMA; IX. and X., MANSFIELD PARK.

AUTHORS for the POCKET.
Choice Passages, mostly selected by A. H. HYATT. 16mo, cloth, 2s. 6d. net each : leather, 4s. net each.
The Pocket R. L. S.
The Pocket George Borrow.
The Pocket Thackeray.
The Pocket Charles Dickens.
The Pocket Richard Jefferies.
The Pocket George MacDonald.
The Pocket Emerson.
The Pocket Thomas Hardy.
The Pocket George Eliot.
The Pocket Charles Kingsley.
The Pocket Lord Beaconsfield.
The Flower of the Mind.

AUZIAS - TURENNE (RAYMOND).—The Last of the Mammoths:
A Romance. Cr. 8vo, cl., 3s. 6d. net.

AYSCOUGH (JOHN), Novels by.
Crown 8vo, cloth, 6s. net. each.

Jacqueline. | **Hurdcott.** | **Faustula.**

Crown 8vo, cloth, 3s. 6d. net each.
Prodigals and Sons.
Outsiders—and In.
Mezzogiorno.
Monksbridge.

Marotz. Crown 8vo, cloth, 2s. net.

BAILDON (H. B.). — Robert Louis Stevenson:
A Study. With 2 Portraits. Crown 8vo, buckram, 5s. net.

BALLADS and LYRICS of LOVE,
selected from PERCY'S 'Reliques.' Edited with an Introduction by F. SIDGWICK. With 10 Plates in Colour after BYAM SHAW, R.I. Large fcap. 4to, cloth, 6s. net.

Legendary Ballads, selected from PERCY'S 'Reliques.' Edited with an Introduction by F. SIDGWICK. With 10 Plates in Colour after BYAM SHAW, R.I. Large fcap. 4to, cloth, 6s. net.

*** The above 2 volumes may also be had in the ST. MARTIN'S LIBRARY, pott 8vo, cloth, 2s. 6d. net each; leather, gilt top, 4s. net each.

BARDSLEY (Rev. C. W.).—English Surnames:
Their Sources and Significations. Cr. 8vo, cloth, 6s. net.

BARING-GOULD (S.), Novels by.
Cr. 8vo, cloth, 3s. 6d. net each; POPULAR EDITIONS, medium 8vo, 9d. net each.

Red Spider. | **Eve.**

BARR (ROBERT), Stories by.
Crown 8vo, cloth, 3s. 6d. net each.

In a Steamer Chair. With 2 Illusts.

From Whose Bourne, &c. With 47 Illustrations by HAL HURST and others.

A Woman Intervenes.

A Prince of Good Fellows. With 15 Illustrations by E. J. SULLIVAN.

The Unchanging East.

The Speculations of John Steele. Crown 8vo, cloth, 3s. 6d. net ; POPULAR EDITION, medium 8vo, 9d. net.

2

BARRETT (FRANK), Novels by.

Cr. 8vo, cloth, 3s. 6d. net each.

Found Guilty. | Folly Morrison.
For Love and Honour.
Between Life and Death.
Fettered for Life.
A Missing Witness. With 8 Illusts.
The Woman of the Iron Bracelets.
The Harding Scandal.
A Prodigal's Progress.
Under a Strange Mask. 19 Illusts.
Was She Justified? | Lady Judas.
The Obliging Husband.
Perfidious Lydia. With Frontispiece.
The Error of Her Ways.
John Ford; and His Helpmate.

POPULAR EDITIONS. Medium 8vo, 9d. net each.
Fettered for Life.
Found Guilty.

BARRINGTON (MICHAEL),
The Knight of the Golden Sword.
Crown 8vo, cloth, 6s. net.

BASKERVILLE (JOHN). By
RALPH STRAUS and R. K. DENT. With
13 Plates. Quarto, buckram, 21s. net.

BAYEUX TAPESTRY, The Book
of the. By HILAIRE BELLOC. With 76
facsimile Coloured Illustrations. Royal
8vo, cloth, 10s. 6d. net.

BEACONSFIELD, LORD. By T.
P. O'CONNOR, M.P. Cr. 8vo, cloth, 5s. net.
The Pocket Beaconsfield. 16mo,
cloth, 2s. 6d. net ; leather gilt top, 4s. net.

BENNETT (ARNOLD), Novels
by. Crown 8vo, cloth, 3s. 6d. net each.
Leonora.
Teresa of Watling Street.
Tales of the Five Towns. | Hugo.
Sacred and Profane Love.
The Gates of Wrath.
The Ghost.
The City of Pleasure.
The Grand Babylon Hotel.

Leonora. POPULAR EDITION, 2s. net.

POPULAR EDITIONS, medium 8vo, 9d. net. each.
The Grand Babylon Hotel.
The City of Pleasure.
Hugo.
Sacred and Profane Love.
A Great Man. | Leonora.

Crown 8vo, cloth, 5s. net.
Books and Persons.
See also under ATKINS (J. B.), p. 2.

BELL (CLIVE). Art : a Critical
Essay. With 6 Illustrations. Cr. 8vo,
buckram, 5s. net.
Books and Pictures. Crown 8vo,
cloth, 6s. net.

BELLOC (HILAIRE). The Book
of the Bayeux Tapestry. With 76
facsimile Coloured Illustrations. Royal
8vo cloth, 10s. 6d. net.

The Conditions of Victory. Small
crown 8vo, coloured wrapper, 1s. net.

BESANT and RICE, Novels by.

Crown 8vo, cloth, 3s. 6d. net each.

Ready-Money Mortiboy.
The Golden Butterfly.
My Little Girl.
With Harp and Crown.
This Son of Vulcan.
The Monks of Thelema.
By Celia's Arbour.
The Chaplain of the Fleet.
The Seamy Side.
The Case of Mr. Lucraft.
'Twas in Trafalgar's Bay.
The Ten Years' Tenant.

BESANT (Sir WALTER),
Novels by. Cr. 8vo, cloth, 3s. net
each.

All Sorts and Conditions of Men.
With 12 Illustrations by FRED. BARNARD.
The Captains' Room, &c.
All in a Garden Fair. With 6 Illus-
trations by HARRY FURNISS.
Dorothy Forster. With Frontispiece.
Uncle Jack, and other Stories.
Children of Gibeon.
The World Went Very Well Then.
With 12 Illustrations by A. FORESTIER.
Herr Paulus.
The Bell of St. Paul's.
For Faith and Freedom. With
Illusts. by A. FORESTIER and F. WADDY.
To Call Her Mine, &c. With 9 Illusts.
The Holy Rose, &c. With Frontispiece.
Armorel of Lyonesse. With 12 Illusts.
St. Katherine's by the Tower.
With 12 Illustrations by C. GREEN.
Verbena Camellia Stephanotis.
The Ivory Gate.
The Rebel Queen.
Beyond the Dreams of Avarice.
With 12 Illustrations by W. H. HYDE.
In Deacon's Orders, &c. With Frontis.
The Revolt of Man.
The Master Craftsman.
The City of Refuge.
A Fountain Sealed.
The Changeling.
The Fourth Generation.
The Orange Girl. With 8 Illustrations
by F. PEGRAM.
The Alabaster Box.
The Lady of Lynn. With 12 Illustra-
tions by G. DEMAIN-HAMMOND.
No Other Way. With 12 Illustrations.

BESANT (Sir Walter)—*continued.*
FINE PAPER EDITIONS, pott 8vo, cloth gilt,
2s. 6d. net each; leather gilt top, 4s.
net each.
London.
Westminster.
Jerusalem. (In collaboration with Prof.
E. H. PALMER.)
Sir Richard Whittington.
Gaspard de Coligny.
All Sorts and Conditions of Men.

POPULAR EDITIONS, med. 8vo, 9d. net each.

All Sorts and Conditions of Men.
The Golden Butterfly.
Ready-Money Mortiboy.
By Celia's Arbour.
The Chaplain of the Fleet.
The Monks of Thelema.
The Orange Girl.
For Faith and Freedom.
Children of Gibeon.
Dorothy Forster.
No Other Way.
Armorel of Lyonesse.
The Lady of Lynn.
My Little Girl.

Demy 8vo, cloth, 6s. net each.
London. With 125 Illustrations.
Westminster. With Etching by F. S.
WALKER, and 130 Illustrations.
South London. With Etching by F. S.
WALKER, and 118 Illustrations.
East London. With Etching by F. S.
WALKER, and 56 Illustrations by PHIL
MAY, L. RAVEN HILL, and J. PENNELL.

Art of Fiction. Fcap. 8vo, cloth, 1s. net.

BIERCE (AMBROSE).—In the
Midst of Life. Crown 8vo, cloth, 3s. 6d.
net; crown 8vo, picture cover, 1s. net.

BINDLOSS (HAROLD), Novels by.
Crown 8vo, cloth, 3s. 6d. net each.
The Mistress of Bonaventure.
Daventry's Daughter.
A Sower of Wheat.
The Concession-hunters.
Ainslie's Ju-ju.

POPULAR EDITIONS, med. 8vo, 9d. net each.
The Concession-hunters.
The Mistress of Bonaventure.

BLAKE (WILLIAM): A Critical
Study by A. C. SWINBURNE. With a
Portrait. Crown 8vo, buckram, 6s. net.
The Marriage of Heaven and
Hell, and A Song of Liberty. With
Introduction by F. G. STOKES. A FLOR-
ENCE PRESS BOOK. Cr. 8vo, hand-made
paper, bds., 3s. 6d. net; parchmt., 5s. net.

BOCCACCIO.—The Decameron.
With a Portrait. Pott 8vo, cloth, 2s. 6d.
net; leather, gilt top, 4s. net.
(*See also under* FLORENCE PRESS BOOKS.)

BOHEMIA'S CLAIM FOR
FREEDOM.—Edit. by J. PROCHAZKA.
With an Introduction by G. K. CHES-
TERTON. Illust. Post 8vo, paper, 1s. net.

BORENIUS (TANCRED).—The
Painters of Vicenza. With 15 full-
page Plates. Demy 8vo., cloth, 7s. 6d. net.

BORROW (GEORGE), The
Pocket. Arranged by EDW. THOMAS.
16mo, cloth 2s. 6d. net; leather,
gilt top, 4s. net.

BOSSES AND CORBELS OF
EXETER CATHEDRAL. By E. K.
PRIDEAUX and G. R. HOLT SHAFTO.
With Illusts. Dy. 8vo, cl., 7s. 6d. net.

BOURGET (PAUL).—The Night
Cometh. Translated by FREDERIC LEES.
Cr. 8vo, cloth, 6s. net.

BRAND (JOHN).—Observations
on Popular Antiquities. With the
Additions of Sir HENRY ELLIS. Crown
8vo, cloth, 3s. 6d. net.

BRANFORD (BENCHARA). —
Janus and Vesta. Crown 8vo, cloth,
6s. net.

BREWER'S (Rev. Dr.) Diction-
ary.
The Reader's Handbook of Famous
Names in Fiction, Allusions,
References, Proverbs, Plots,
Stories, and Poems. Crown 8vo,
cloth, 5s. net.

BRIDGE CATECHISM: QUES-
TIONS AND ANSWERS: including
the PORTLAND CLUB CODE. By ROBERT
HAMMOND. Fcap. 8vo, cloth, 2s. 6d. net.

BRIDGE (J. S. C.).—From Island
to Empire: A History of the Expansion of
England by Force of Arms. With Maps
and Plans. Large crown 8vo, cl., 6s. net;
also crown 8vo, cloth, 2s. net.

BROWNING'S (ROBT.) POEMS.
Large fcap. 4to, cl., 6s. net ea.; LARGE PAPER
EDITION, parchment, 12s. 6d. net each.—
Also in the ST. MARTIN'S LIBRARY, pott 8vo,
cloth, 2s. 6d. net each; leather, gilt top,
4s. net each.

4

BROWNING'S (ROBT.) POEMS—*contd.*

Pippa Passes; and **Men and Women.** With 10 Plates in Colour after E. FORTESCUE BRICKDALE. No parchment copies.

Dramatis Personæ; and **Dramatic Romances and Lyrics.** With 10 Plates in Colour after E. F. BRICKDALE.

Browning's Heroines. By ETHEL COLBURN MAYNE. Cr. 8vo, cloth, 6s. net.

BUCHANAN (ROBERT), Poems and Novels by.

The Complete Poetical Works of Robert Buchanan. 2 Vols., crown 8vo, buckram, with Portrait Frontispiece to each volume, 12s. net.

Crown 8vo, cloth, 3s. 6d. net each.

The Shadow of the Sword.
A Child of Nature.
God and the Man. With 11 Illustrations by F. BARNARD.
Lady Kilpatrick.
The Martyrdom of Madeline.
Love Me for Ever.
Annan Water.
Foxglove Manor.
The New Abelard.
Rachel Dene.
Matt: A Story of a Caravan.
The Master of the Mine.
The Heir of Linne.
Woman and the Man.
Red and White Heather.
Andromeda.

POPULAR EDITIONS, med. 8vo, 9d. net each.

The Shadow of the Sword.
God and the Man.
Foxglove Manor.
The Martyrdom of Madeline.

The Shadow of the Sword. FINE PAPER EDITION. Pott 8vo, cloth, 2s. 6d. net; leather, gilt top, 4s. net.

The Charlatan. By ROBERT BUCHANAN and HENRY MURRAY. Crown 8vo, cloth, 3s. 6d. net.

BURTON (ROBERT). — The Anatomy of Melancholy. With a Frontispiece. Demy 8vo, cloth, 6s. net.

BYRD (JOHN WALTER).—The Born Fool. Crown 8vo, cloth, 6s. net.

BYZANTINE ENAMELS IN MR. PIERPONT MORGAN'S COLLECTION. By O. M. DALTON. With Note by ROGER FRY, and Illustrations in Colour. Royal 4to, boards, 7s. 6d. net.

CAINE (HALL), Novels by.
Crown 8vo, cloth, 3s. 6d. net each.

The Shadow of a Crime.
A Son of Hagar.
The Deemster.
Also POPULAR EDITIONS, picture covers, 9d. net each; and the FINE PAPER EDITION of **The Deemster**, pott 8vo, cloth, 2s. 6d. net; leather, 4s. net.

CAINE (WILLIAM).—Monsieur Segotin's Story. Demy 8vo, coloured wrapper, 3d. net.

CAMBRIDGE FROM WITHIN.
By CHARLES TENNYSON. With 12 Illustrations in Colour and 8 in Sepia by HARRY MORLEY. Demy 8vo, cloth, 5s. net.

CAMERON (V. LOVETT).—The Cruise of the 'Black Prince' Privateer. Cr. 8vo, cloth, with 2 Illusts., 3s. 6d. net.

CANZIANI (ESTELLA), Books by.

Costumes, Traditions, and Songs of Savoy. With 50 Illustrations in Colour and some in Line. Demy 4to, cl. gilt, 21s. net; vellum gilt, 31s. 6d. net.

Piedmont. By ESTELLA CANZIANI and ELEANOUR ROHDE. With 52 Illustrations in Colour and many in Line. Demy 4to, cloth, 21s. net.

CARROLL (LEWIS), Books by.
Alice in Wonderland. With 12 Col. and many Line Illus. by MILLICENT SOWERBY. Large cr. 8vo, cloth, 3s. 6d. net.
Feeding the Mind. With a Preface by W. H. DRAPER. Post 8vo, boards, 1s. net; leather, 2s. net.

CATHOLICITY, WHAT IS?—
Letters from the *Church Times* and the *Tablet*, Collected by W. W. Crown 8vo, paper, 1s. net.

CHAPMAN'S (GEORGE) Works.
Vol. I., Plays Complete, including the Doubtful Ones.—Vol. II., Poems and Minor Translations, with Essay by A. C. SWINBURNE.—Vol. III., Translations of the Iliad and Odyssey. Three Vols., crown 8vo, cloth, 3s. 6d. net each.

CHAUCER for Children: A Golden Key. By Mrs. H. R. HAWEIS. With 8 Coloured Plates and 30 Woodcuts. Crown 4to, cloth, 3s. 6d. net.

Chaucer for Schools. With the Story of his Times and his Work. By Mrs. H. R. HAWEIS. Demy 8vo, cl., 2s. 6d. net.

. See also THE KING'S CLASSICS, p. 16.

CHESNEY (WEATHERBY), Novels by. Cr. 8vo, cl., 3s. 6d. net each.
The Cable-man.
The Claimant.
The Romance of a Queen.

CHESS, The Laws and Practice of; with an Analysis of the Openings. By HOWARD STAUNTON. Edited by R. B. WORMALD. Crown 8vo, cl., 5s. net.

The Minor Tactics of Chess: A Treatise on the Deployment of the Forces in obedience to Strategic Principle. By F. K. YOUNG and E. C. HOWELL. Long fcap. 8vo, cloth, 2s. 6d. net.

The Hastings Chess Tournament, Aug.-Sept. 1895. With Annotations by PILLSBURY, LASKER, TARRASCH, STEINITZ, SCHIFFERS, TEICHMANN, BARDELEBEN, BLACKBURNE, GUNSBERG, TINSLEY, MASON and ALBIN; also Biographies and Portraits. Edited by H. F. CHESHIRE. Crown 8vo, cloth, 5s. net.

CHESTERTON (G. K.).—A Short History of England. Crown 8vo, cloth, 5s. net.

CHRISTMAS CAROLS, ANCIENT ENGLISH. Collected and arranged by EDITH RICKERT. Post 8vo, cloth, 3s. 6d. net. Parchment, 5s. net. See also NEW MEDIEVAL LIBRARY, p 19.

CLAUDEL (PAUL).—The Tidings Brought to Mary. Translated by LOUISE MORGAN SILL. Pott 4to, cloth, 6s. net.

CLODD (EDWARD). — Myths and Dreams. Cr. 8vo, cloth, 3s. 6d. net.

COLLINS (J. CHURTON, M.A.). Jonathan Swift. Cr. 8vo, cl., 3s. 6d. net.

COLLINS (WILKIE), Novels by. Cr. 8vo, cl., 3s. 6d. net each.
Antonina.
Basil.
Hide and Seek.
The Woman in White.
The Moonstone.
Man and Wife.
The Dead Secret.
After Dark.
The Queen of Hearts.
No Name.
My Miscellanies.
Armadale.
Poor Miss Finch.
Miss or Mrs.?
The Black Robe.
The New Magdalen.
Frozen Deep.
A Rogue's Life.
The Law and the Lady.
The Two Destinies.
The Haunted Hotel.
The Fallen Leaves.
Jezebel's Daughter.
Heart and Science. | "I Say No."
The Evil Genius. | Little Novels.
The Legacy of Cain. | Blind Love.

POPULAR EDITIONS, medium 8vo, 9d. net each.
Antonina.
Poor Miss Finch.
The Woman in White.
The Law and the Lady.
Moonstone.
The New Magdalen.
The Dead Secret.
Man and Wife.
No Name.
Armadale.
The Haunted Hotel.
Blind Love.
The Legacy of Cain.

The Woman in White. LARGE TYPE, FINE PAPER EDITION. Pott 8vo, cloth, gilt top, 2s. 6d. net; leather, gilt top, 4s. net.

The Frozen Deep. LARGE TYPE EDIT. Fcap. 8vo, cloth, 1s. net.

COLVILL (HELEN H.). — The Incubus. Crown 8vo, cloth, 6s. net.

COMPENSATION ACT (THE), 1906. By A. CLEMENT EDWARDS, M.P. Crown 8vo, cloth, 1s. 6d. net.

COMPTON (HERBERT), Novels by.

The Inimitable Mrs. Massingham. POPULAR EDITION, med. 8vo, 9*d*. net.

Crown 8vo, cloth, 3*s*. 6*d*. net each.

The Wilful Way.
The Queen can do no Wrong.
To Defeat the Ends of Justice.

CORNWALL.—Popular Romances of the West of England: Collected by ROBERT HUNT, F.R.S. With two Plates by GEORGE CRUIKSHANK. Cr. 8vo, cloth, 6*s*. net.

CREIGHTON (BASIL). — The History of an Attraction. Crown 8vo, cloth, 5*s*. net.

CRESSWELL (C. M.) — The Making and Breaking of Almansur. Crown 8vo, cloth, 6*s*. net.

CROSS (MARGARET B.), Novels by. Crown 8vo, cloth, 6*s*. net each.

Opportunity.
Up to Perrin's.

A Question of Means. Cr. 8vo, cl., 3*s*. 6*d*. POPULAR EDITION, medium 8vo, 9*d*. net.

CRUIKSHANK'S COMIC AL- MANACK. Complete in TWO SERIES: the FIRST from 1835 to 1843; the SECOND, from 1844 to 1853. With many hundred Woodcuts and Steel Plates by GEORGE CRUIKSHANK and others. Two Vols., crown 8vo, cloth, 5*s*. net each.

CROKER (B. M.), Novels by. Cr. 8vo, cloth, 3*s*. 6*d*. net each.

A Bird of Passage.
Mr. Jervis.
Diana Barrington.
"To Let."
A Family Likeness.
Terence.
A Third Person.
Interference.
Beyond the Pale.
Two Masters.
Infatuation.
Some One Else.
In the Kingdom of Kerry.
Jason, &c.
Married or Single?

CROKER (B. M.)—*continued*.

Miss Balmaine's Past.
Pretty Miss Neville.
Proper Pride. | The Cat's-paw.
The Real Lady Hilda.
The Spanish Necklace.
Village Tales & Jungle Tragedies.
A Rolling Stone.

POPULAR EDITIONS, med. 8vo. 9*d* net each.

Proper Pride | The Cat's-paw.
Diana Barrington.
A Bird of Passage.
A Family Likeness.
The Spanish Necklace.
A Rolling Stone. | Infatuation.
Pretty Miss Neville.
Beyond the Pale.
The Real Lady Hilda.
Married or Single?

CUPID AND PSYCHE. With 8 Illustrations in colour by DOROTHY MULLOCK. Fcap. 4to, boards, 5*s*. net.

CUSSANS (JOHN E.).—A Hand- book of Heraldry. With 408 Woodcuts and 2 Colrd. Plates. Cr. 8vo, cl., 5*s*. net.

DAVIES (Dr. N. E. YORKE-). Crown 8vo, 1*s*. net ; cloth, 1*s*. 6*d*. net.

The Dietetic Cure of Obesity (Foods for the Fat).

Aids to Long Life. Cr. 8vo, 2*s*. net; cl. 2*s*. 6*d*. net.

Crown 8vo, cloth, 1*s*. 6*d*. net.

Wine and Health : How to enjoy both.

One Thousand Medical Maxims and Surgical Hints.

Nursery Hints : A Mother's Guide.

DELSTANCHE (ALBERT).—The Little Towns of Flanders. Twelve Woodcuts, with Prefatory Letter from EMILE VERHAEREN. Fcap. 4to, boards, 3*s*. 6*d*. net. *See also* under FLORENCE PRESS BOOKS, page 10.

DEVON: Its Moorlands, Streams, and Coasts. By Lady ROSALIND NORTHCOTE. Illustrated in Colours by F. J. WIDGERY. Fcap. 4to, cloth, 10*s*. 6*d*. net.

Folk Rhymes of Devon. By W. CROSSING. Demy 8vo, cloth, 4*s*. 6*d*. net.

Lynton and Lynmouth. By JOHN PRESLAND. Illustrated in Colour by F. J. WIDGERY. Crown 8vo, cloth, 7*s*. 6*d*. net.

7

DEWAR (GEORGE A.B.).—This Realm, This England. With 9 Illustrations. Crown 8vo, cloth, 2s. net.

DEWAR (T. R.).—A Ramble Round the Globe. With 220 Illustrations. Crown 8vo, cloth, 6s. net.

DICKENS (CHARLES), The Speeches of. With a Portrait. Pott 8vo, cloth, 2s. 6d. net ; leather, 4s. net.

Charles Dickens. By ALGERNON CHARLES SWINBURNE. Crown 8vo, cloth, 3s. 6d. net.

The Pocket Charles Dickens: Passages chosen by ALFRED H. HYATT. 16mo, cloth, 2s. 6d. net ; leather, gilt top, 4s. net.

DICTIONARIES.

A Dictionary of the Drama. By W. DAVENPORT ADAMS. Vol. I. (A to G) Demy 8vo, cloth 10s. 6d. net.

The Reader's Handbook. By Rev. E. C. BREWER, LL.D. Crown 8vo, cloth, 5s. net.

Familiar Allusions. By W. A. and C. G. WHEELER. Demy 8vo, cl., 7s. 6d. net.

Familiar Short Sayings of Great Men. With Explanatory Notes by SAMUEL A. BENT, A.M. Cr. 8vo, cl., 6s. net.

The Slang Dictionary : Historical and Anecdotal. Crown 8vo, cloth, 6s. net.

Words, Facts, and Phrases: A Dictionary of Curious Matters. By E. EDWARDS. Crown 8vo, cloth, 3s. 6d. net.

DOBSON (AUSTIN), Works by. Crown 8vo, buckram, 5s. net each.

Four Frenchwomen. With Portraits.

Eighteenth Century Vignettes. In Three Series ; also FINE-PAPER EDITIONS, pott 8vo, cloth, 2s. 6d. net each ; leather, 4s. net each.

A Paladin of Philanthropy, and other Papers. With 2 Illustrations.

Side-walk Studies. With 5 Illusts.

Old Kensington Palace, &c. With 6 Illustrations.

At Prior Park, &c. With 6 Illustrations.

Rosalba's Journal 8vo, with 6 Illus.

DIMNET (ERNEST). — France Herself Again. Demy 8vo, cloth, 16s. net.

DIRCKS (HELEN).—FINDING. Pott 8vo, cloth, 2s. 6d. net.

DIXON (W. WILLMOTT), Novels by. Crown 8vo, cloth, 3s. 6d. net each.

The Rogue of Rye.
King Hal of Heronsea.

DONOVAN (DICK), Detective Stories by. Cr. 8vo, cloth, 3s. 6d. net each.

Suspicion Aroused.
In the Grip of the Law.
The Man from Manchester.
The Mystery of Jamaica Terrace.
Wanted !
Chronicles of Michael Danevitch.
Tracked to Doom.
Tracked and Taken.
A Detective's Triumphs.
Who Poisoned Hetty Duncan?
Caught at Last.
Link by Link.
Riddles Read.
From Information Received.
The Man-Hunter.
Tales of Terror.
Deacon Brodie.
Tyler Tatlock, Private Detective.
The Records of Vincent Trill.

DOSTOEVSKY (FYODOR), Letters of. Translated by ETHEL COLBURN MAYNE. With 16 Illustrations. Demy 8vo, buckram, 7s. 6d. net. NEW AND CHEAPER EDITION, reset with all the original illustrations. Crown 8vo, cloth, 6s. n't.

DOYLE (A. CONAN).—The Firm of Girdlestone. Cr. 8vo, cl., 3s. 6d. net ; POPULAR EDITION, medium 8vo, 9d. net.

DRAMATISTS, THE OLD. Edited by Col. CUNNINGHAM. Cr. 8vo, cloth, with Portraits. 3s. 6d. net. per Vol.

Ben Jonson's Works. With Notes and a Biographical Memoir by WILLIAM GIFFORD. Three Vols.

Chapman's Works. Three Vols.—Vol. I. The Plays complete ; Vol. II. Poems and Translations, with Essay by A. C. SWINBURNE ; Vol. III. The Iliad and Odyssey.

Marlowe's Works. One Vol.

Massinger's Plays. One Vol.

DRAPER (W. H.). — Poems of the Love of England. Crown 8vo, Decorated cover, 1s. net.

(*See also under* PETRARCH.)

DU MAURIER (GEORGE), The Satirist of the Victorians. By T. MARTIN WOOD. With 41 Illustrations. Fcap. 4to, cloth, 7s. 6d. net.

8

DUMPY BOOKS (The) for Children. Royal 32mo, cloth, 1s. net each.

1. **The Flamp, The Ameliorator, and The School-boy's Apprentice.** By E. V. LUCAS.

4. **The Story of Little Black Sambo.** By HELEN BANNERMAN. Illustrated in colours.

7. **A Flower Book.** Illustrated in colours by NELLIE BENSON.

8. **The Pink Knight.** By J. R. MONSELL. Illustrated in colours.

9. **The Little Clown.** By T. COBB.

10. **A Horse Book.** By MARY TOURTEL. Illustrated in colours.

11. **Little People:** an Alphabet. By HENRY MAYER and T. W. H. CROSLAND. Illustrated in colours.

12. **A Dog Book.** By ETHEL BICKNELL. With Pictures in colours by CARTON MOORE PARK.

15. **Dollies.** By RICHARD HUNTER. Illustrated in colours by RUTH COBB.

17 **Peter Piper's Practical Principles.** Illustrated in colours.

18. **Little White Barbara.** By ELEANOR MARCH. Illustrated in colours.

22. **The Old Man's Bag.** By T. W. H. CROSLAND. Illus. by J. R. MONSELL.

25. **More Dollies.** By RICHARD HUNTER. Illus. in colours by RUTH COBB.

28. **The Sooty Man.** By E. B. MACKINNON and EDEN COYBEE. Illus.

30. **Rosalina.** Illustrated in colours by JEAN C. ARCHER.

31. **Sammy and the Snarlywink.** Illustrated in colours by LENA and NORMAN AULT.

33. **Irene's Christmas Party.** By RICHARD HUNTER. Illus. by RUTH COBB.

34. **The Little Soldier Book.** By JESSIE POPE. Illustrated in colours by HENRY MAYER.

35. **The Dutch Doll's Ditties.** By C. AUBREY MOORE.

36. **Ten Little Nigger Boys.** By NORA CASE.

37. **Humpty Dumpty's Little Son.** By HELEN R. CROSS.

38. **Simple Simon.** By HELEN R. CROSS. Illustrated in colours.

39. **The Little Frenchman.** By EDEN COYBEE. Illustrated in colours by K. J. FRICERO.

40. **The Story of an Irish Potato.** By LILY SCHOFIELD. Illust. in colours.

DUTT (ROMESH C.).—England and India: Progress during One Hundred Years. Crown 8vo, cl., 2s. net.

EDWARDS (ELIEZER).— Words, Facts, and Phrases: A Dictionary of Curious, Quaint, and Out-of-the-Way Matters. Cr. 8vo, cloth, 3s. 6d. net.

EGERTON (Rev. J. C.).— Sussex Folk and Sussex Ways. With Four Illusts. Cr. 8vo, cl., 3s. 6d. net.

ELIZABETHAN VERSE, The Book of. Edited, with Notes, by W. S. BRAITHWAITE. Crown 8vo, cloth, 3s. 6d. net; vellum gilt, 12s. 6d. net.

EPISTOLÆ OBSCURORUM Virorum (1515-1517). Latin Text, with Translation, Notes, &c., by F. G. STOKES. Royal 8vo, buckram, 25s. net.

EXETER SCHOOL, The Founding of. By H. LLOYD PARRY. Crown 4to, cloth, 5s. net.

FAIRY TALES FROM TUSCANY. By ISABELLA M. ANDERTON. Square 16mo, cloth, 1s. net.

FAMILIAR ALLUSIONS Miscellaneous Information. By W. A. and C. G. WHEELER. Demy 8vo, cl., 7s. 6d. net.

FAMILIAR SHORT SAYINGS of Great Men. By S. A. BENT, A.M. Crown 8vo, cloth, 6s. net.

FARADAY (MICHAEL), Works by. Post 8vo, cloth, 3s. 6d. net each.

The Chemical History of a Candle: Lectures delivered before a Juvenile Audience. Edited by WILLIAM CROOKES, F.C.S. With numerous Illusts.

On the Various Forces of Nature, and their Relations to each other. Edited by WILLIAM CROOKES, F.C.S. With Illustrations.

FARMER (HENRY).—Slaves of Chance: A Novel. Cr. 8vo, cloth, 6s. net.

FARRAR (F. W., D.D.).—Ruskin as a Religious Teacher. Square 16mo, cloth, with Frontispiece, 1s. net.

FENN (G. MANVILLE), Novels by. Crown 8vo, cloth, 3s. 6d. net each.

The New Mistress.
Witness to the Deed.
The Tiger Lily.
The White Virgin.
A Woman Worth Winning.
Cursed by a Fortune.
The Case of Ailsa Gray.
Commodore Junk.
In Jeopardy.
Double Cunning.
A Fluttered Dovecote.
King of the Castle.
The Master of the Ceremonies.
The Story of Antony Grace.
The Man with a Shadow.
One Maid's Mischief.
The Bag of Diamonds, and Three Bits of Paste.
Black Shadows.
Running Amok.
The Cankerworm.
So Like a Woman.
A Crimson Crime.

POPULAR EDITIONS. med. 8vo, 9d. net each.

A Crimson Crime.
A Woman Worth Winning.

FILIPPI (ROSINA).—Inhaling:
A Romance. Crown 8vo, cloth, 6s. net.

FIREWORK - MAKING, The
Complete Art of. By T. KENTISH. With 267 Illusts. Cr. 8vo, cl., 3s. 6d. net.

FISHER (ARTHUR O.).—The
Land of Silent Feet. With a Frontispiece by G. D. ARMOUR. Crown 8vo, cloth, 6s. net.

FLAMMARION (CAMILLE).—
Popular Astronomy. Translated by J. ELLARD GORE, F.R.A.S. With Illustrations. Medium 8vo, cloth, 10s. 6d. net.

FLOWER BOOK (The). By
CONSTANCE SMEDLEY ARMFIELD and MAXWELL ARMFIELD. Large fcap 4to, cl., 5s. net.

FLORENCE PRESS BOOKS
(The). Set in the beautiful FLORENCE TYPE designed by Mr. HERBERT P. HORNE. Printed on hand-made paper,

FLORENCE PRESS BOOKS—continued.

Virginibus Puerisque, &c. By R. L. STEVENSON. With 12 Illustrations in Coloured Collotype after the Drawings of NORMAN WILKINSON (235 numbered copies.) Crown 4to, bds., £2 12s. 6d net ; vellum, £3 3s. net.

The Fioretti or Little Flowers of S. Francis. Translated by Prof. T. W. ARNOLD, M.A. With 29 Illustrations in Collotype from the MSS. in the Laurentian Library. (475 numbered Copies.) Printed in red and black. Demy 4to, boards, 30s. net ; vellum, 42s. net.

Songs before Sunrise. By ALGERNON CHARLES SWINBURNE. (475 numbered copies.) Printed in red and black. Crown 4to, boards, 26s. net ; limp vellum, 36s. net.

The Marriage of Heaven and Hell ; and A Song of Liberty. By WILLIAM BLAKE. With Introduction by F. G. STOKES. Crown 8vo, boards, 3s. 6d. net ; parchment 5s. net.

Sappho: One Hundred Lyrics. By BLISS CARMAN. Small crown 8vo, boards, 5s. net ; parchment gilt, 6s. net.

Memoriale di Molte Statue e Pitture, Sono Inclyta Cipta di Florentia. (Edition limited to 450 copies.) Demy 8vo, 5s. net ; limp vellum, 12s. 6d. net.

Olympia: The Latin Text of Boccaccio's Fourteenth Eclogue, with an English rendering, and other supplementary matter, by ISRAEL GOLLANCZ, Litt.D., and a Photogravure facsimile of a part of the MS. Limited to 500 copies fcap. 4to, hand-made paper, boards, 6s. net ; vellum, 12s. 6d. net.

Stevenson's Poems. Complete Edition. Small fcap. 4to, gilt top, 12s. 6d. net.

The Poems of John Keats. Newly arranged in chronological order, and Edited by Sir SIDNEY COLVIN. In 2 vols., small 4to, boards, 15s. net ; buckram, 21s. net. LARGE PAPER EDITION, limited to 250 copies, fcap. 4to, hand-made paper, parchment, 31s. 6d net ; vellum, 45s. net.

The Lyrical Poems of Shelley. Newly Edited by Prof. C. H. HERFORD. 1 Vol. small 4to, boards, 12s. 6d. net ; buckram, 16s. net. Also a LARGE PAPER EDITION, limited to 250 numbered copies. Parchment, 25s. net.

Flanders, The Little Towns of. 18 Woodcuts by ALBERT DELSTANCHE, with a Prefatory Letter from EMILE VERHAEREN. Edition limited to 500 numbered copies. Demy 4to, bds., 12s. 6d. net ; vellum, £1 1s. net.

FRANKAU (GILBERT).—One of
Us : A Novel in Verse. Crown 8vo, paper, 1s. net. Special Edition with Illustrations by "FISH." Fcap. 4to, boards, 5s. net. 100 copies bound in parchment and signed by the Author and Artist, 12s. 6d. net. Only a few remain.

"Tid'Apa": A Poem. Demy 8vo, boards, 2s. 6d. net.

The City of Fear. Pott 4to, cloth, 3s. 6d. net.

The Judgement of Valhalla. Pott 4to, cloth, 3s. 6d. net.

The Woman of the Horizon. Crown 8vo, cloth, 6s. net.

FREEMAN (R. AUSTIN).—John Thorndyke's Cases. Illustrated by H. M. BROCK, &c. POPULAR EDITION, medium 8vo, 9d. net.

FRY'S (HERBERT) Royal Guide to the London Charities. Edited by JOHN LANE. Published Annually. Crown 8vo, cloth, 1s. 6d. net.

FRY (ROGER).—Children's Pictures and the Teaching of Art. Illustrated in Colour and Monochrome. Fcap. 4to, boards, 2s. 6d. net.

GARDENING BOOKS. Post 8vo, 1s. 6d. net each.

A Year's Work in Garden and Greenhouse. By GEORGE GLENNY. Also an edition at 1s. net.

Household Horticulture. By TOM and JANE JERROLD. Illustrated.

The Garden that Paid the Rent. By TOM JERROLD.

Our Kitchen Garden. By TOM JERROLD. Post 8vo, cloth, 1s. net.

GIBBON (CHARLES), Novels by. Crown 8vo, cloth, 3s. 6d. net each.

Robin Gray.
The Golden Shaft.
The Flower of the Forest.
The Braes of Yarrow.
Of High Degree.
Queen of the Meadow.
By Mead and Stream.
For Lack of Gold.

The Dead Heart. POPULAR EDITION, medium 8vo, 9d. net.

GIBBS (A. HAMILTON).— Cheadle and Son. Crown 8vo, cloth, 6s. net.

GIBSON (L. S.), Novels by. Crown 8vo, cloth, 3s. 6d. net each.

The Freemasons.
Burnt Spices.
Ships of Desire.

The Freemasons. Cheap Edition, medium 8vo, 9d. net.

GILBERT'S (W. S.) Original Plays. In 4 Series, FINE-PAPER EDITION, Post 8vo, cloth 2s. 6d. net each; leather, gilt top, 4s. net each.

The FIRST SERIES contains: The Wicked World — Pygmalion and Galatea — Charity — The Princess — The Palace of Truth — Trial by Jury — Iolanthe.

The SECOND SERIES contains: Broken Hearts — Engaged — Sweethearts — Gretchen — Dan'l Druce — Tom Cobb — H.M.S. 'Pinafore' — The Sorcerer — The Pirates of Penzance.

The THIRD SERIES contains: Comedy and Tragedy — Foggerty's Fairy — Rosencrantz and Guildenstern — Patience — Princess Ida — The Mikado - Ruddigore — The Yeomen of the Guard — The Gondoliers — The Mountebanks — Utopia.

The FOURTH SERIES contains: The Fairy's Dilemma — The Grand Duke - His Excellency — 'Haste to the Wedding — Fallen Fairies — The Gentleman in Black — Brantinghame Hall — Creatures of Impulse — Randall's Thumb — The Fortune-hunter — Thespis. With Portrait of the Author.

Eight Original Comic Operas. Two Series, demy 8vo, cl., 2s. 6d. net each.

The FIRST SERIES contains: The Sorcerer — H.M.S. 'Pinafore' — The Pirates of Penzance — Iolanthe — Patience — Princess Ida — The Mikado — Trial by Jury.

The SECOND SERIES contains: The Gondoliers — The Grand Duke — The Yeomen of the Guard — His Excellency — Utopia, Limited — Ruddigore — The Mountebanks — Haste to the Wedding.

The Gilbert and Sullivan Birthday Book. Compiled by A. WATSON. Royal 16mo, decorated cover, 1s. net.

GISSING (ALGERNON), Novels by. Cr. 8vo, cloth, 3s. 6d. net each.
Knitters in the Sun.
The Wealth of Mallerstang.
An Angel's Portion. | Baliol Garth
The Dreams of Simon Usher.

GLANVILLE (ERNEST), Novels by. Crown 8vo, cloth, 3s. 6d. net each.
The Lost Heiress. With 2 Illusts.
The Fossicker: A Romance of Mashonaland. Two Illusts. by HUME NISBET.
A Fair Colonist. With Frontispiece.
The Golden Rock. With Frontispiece.
Tales from the Veld. With 12 Illusts.
Max Thornton. With 8 Illustrations by J. S. CROMPTON, R.I.

GOLDEN TREASURY of Thought, The. By THEODORE TAYLOR. Cr. 8vo, cl., 3s. 6d. net.

GRACE (ALFRED A.).—Tales of a Dying Race. Cr. 8vo, cloth, 3s. 6d. net.

GRACE, E. M.: A Memoir. By F. S. ASHLEY-COOPER. Crown 8vo, cloth, 5s. net.

GRANDE (JULIAN). — A Citizens' Army: The Swiss Military System. Cr. 8vo, cloth, 3s. 6d. net.

GREEKS AND ROMANS, The Life of the. By ERNST GUHL and W. KONER. Edited by Dr. F. HUEFFER. With 545 Illusts. Demy 8vo, cl., 6s. net.

GREEN (ARTHUR).—The Story of a Prisoner of War. Pott 8vo, 1s. net.

GREEN (F. E.) — The Surrey Hills. Illustrated by ELLIOTT SEABROOKE. Fcap. 4to, cloth, 7s. 6d. net.

GRIMM. — German Popular Stories. — Collected by the Brothers GRIMM and Translated by EDGAR TAYLOR. With an Intro. by JOHN RUSKIN. Illustrated by GEORGE CRUIKSHANK. Square 8vo, cloth, gilt top, 5s. net.

HABBERTON (JOHN).—Helen's Babies. With Coloured Frontis. and 60 Illustrations by EVA ROOS. Fcap. 4to, cloth, 6s. net.

HALL (Mrs. S. C.).—Sketches of Irish Character. Illusts. by CRUIKSHANK and others. Demy 8vo, cl., 6s. net.

HAMILTON'S (COSMO) Stories

Two Kings, &c. Cr. 8vo., cl., 2s. net.

Crown 8vo, cloth, 6s. net. each.
Nature's Vagabond, &c.
The Door that has no Key.

HAMILTON'S (COSMO) Stories— continued.

Plain Brown. Cr. 8vo, cloth, 3s. 6d. net.

POPULAR EDITION, medium 8vo, 9d. net.

A Plea for the Younger Generation. Crown 8vo, cloth, 2s. 6d. net.

HAPPY TESTAMENT, The. By CHARLES LOUNDSBERRY. Illustrated in Colour by RACHEL MARSHALL. Post 8vo, decorated cover, 1s. net.

HAPSBURGS, The Cradle of the. By J. W. GILBART-SMITH, M.A. With numerous Illusts. Cr. 8vo, cloth, 5s. net.

HARDY (THOMAS). — Under the Greenwood Tree. Post 8vo, cloth, 3s. 6d. net; FINE PAPER EDITION, pott 8vo, cloth, 2s. 6d. net; leather gilt, 4s. net; CHEAP EDITION, medium 8vo, 9d. net. Also the LARGE TYPE EDITION DE LUXE, with 10 Illustrations in Colour by KEITH HENDERSON. Fcap. 4to, cloth, 3s. 6d. net.

The Pocket Thomas Hardy. 16mo, cloth, 2s. 6d. net; leather, gilt top, 4s. net.

HARRIS (JOEL CHANDLER):

Uncle Remus. With 9 Coloured and 50 other Illustrations by J. A. SHEPHERD. Fcap. 4to, cloth, 6s. net.

Nights with Uncle Remus. With 8 Coloured and 50 other Illustrations by J. A. SHEPHERD. Fcap. 4to, cl. 6s. net.

HARTE'S (BRET) Collected Works. LIBRARY EDITION. (Ten Volumes now ready). Crown 8vo, cloth, 3s. 6d. net each.

Vol. I. POETICAL AND DRAMATIC WORKS. With Portrait.

„ II. THE LUCK OF ROARING CAMP—BOHEMIAN PAPERS—AMERICAN LEGENDS.

„ III. TALES OF THE ARGONAUTS—EASTERN SKETCHES.

„ IV. GABRIEL CONROY.

„ V. STORIES — CONDENSED NOVELS.

„ VI. TALES OF THE PACIFIC SLOPE.

„ VII. TALES OF THE PACIFIC SLOPE—II. With Portrait by JOHN PETTIE.

„ VIII. TALES OF PINE AND CYPRESS.

„ IX. BUCKEYE AND CHAPARREL.

„ X. TALES OF TRAIL AND TOWN.

HARTE (BRET)—continued.

Bret Harte's Choice Works in Prose and Verse. With Portrait and 40 Illustrations. Crown 8vo, cloth, 3s. 6d. net.

Pott 8vo, cloth, 2s. 6d. net each; leather, 4s. net each.

Mliss, Luck of Roaring Camp, &c.

Condensed Novels. Both Series.

Complete Poetical Works.

Crown 8vo, cloth, 6s. net. each.

On the Old Trail.

Trent's Trust.

Under the Redwoods.

From Sandhill to Pine.

Stories in Light and Shadow.

Mr. Jack Hamlin's Mediation.

Crown 8vo, cloth, 3s. 6d. net each.

In a Hollow of the Hills.

Maruja.

Gabriel Conroy.

A Ward of the Golden Gate. With 59 Illustrations by STANLEY L. WOOD.

The Bell-Ringer of Angel's, &c. With 39 Illusts. by DUDLEY HARDY, &c.

Clarence: A Story of the American War. With 8 Illustrations by A. JULE GOODMAN.

Barker's Luck, &c. With 39 Illustrations by A. FORESTIER, PAUL HARDY, &c.

Devil's Ford, &c.

The Crusade of the 'Excelsior.' With Frontis. by J. BERNARD PARTRIDGE.

Tales of Trail and Town. With Frontispiece by G. P. JACOMB-HOOD.

A Sappho of Green Springs.

Colonel Starbottle's Client.

A Protégée of Jack Hamlin's. With numerous Illustrations.

Sally Dows, &c. With 47 Illustrations by W. D. ALMOND and others.

An Heiress of Red Dog.

Californian Stories.

Luck of Roaring Camp.

Condensed Novels: New Burlesques.

Three Partners. POPULAR EDITION, medium 8vo, 9d. net.

HAWEIS (Mrs. H. R.), Books by.

The Art of Dress. With 32 Illustrations. Post 8vo, cloth, 1s. 6d net.

Chaucer for Schools. With Frontispiece. Demy 8vo, cloth, 2s. 6d. net.

Chaucer for Children. With 8 Coloured Plates and 30 Woodcuts. Crown 4to, cloth, 3s. 6d. net.

HAWTHORNE (JULIAN), Novels by. Crown 8vo, cloth, 3s. 6d. net each.

Garth. | **Ellice Quentin.**
Fortune's Fool. | **Dust.** Four Illusts.
Beatrix Randolph With Four Illusts.
D. Poindexter's Disappearance.
Sebastian Strome.
Love—or a Name.

HEAD (Mrs. HENRY).—A Simple Guide to Pictures. With 34 Illustrations (24 in Colour). Fcap. 4to, cloth, 5s. net.

HEALY (CHRIS), Books by. Crown 8vo, cloth, 6s. net. each.

Confessions of a Journalist.
Heirs of Reuben. | **Mara.**

HENDERSON (KEITH).— Letters to Helen: The Impressions of an Artist on the Western Front. Illustrated. Demy 8vo, boards, 6s. net.

HENTY (G. A.), Novels by.

Rujub, the Juggler. Post 8vo, cloth, 3s 6d. net.

Crown 8vo, cloth, 3s. 6d. net each.

The Queen's Cup.
Dorothy's Double.
Colonel Thorndyke's Secret.

HERBERTSON (JESSIE L.).— Junia. Crown 8vo, cloth, 6s. net.

HILL (HEADON).—Zambra the Detective. Crown 8vo, cloth, 3s. 6d. net.

HOFFMANN (PROF.). — King Koko. A Magic Story. Cr. 8vo, cl., 1s. net

HOFFMANN, TALES OF. Retold from OFFENBACH'S Opera. By CYRIL FALLS. Illustrated in Colour by A. BRANTINGHAM SIMPSON, R.O.I. Small 4to, cl., 3s. 6d. net.

HOLMES (CHARLES J., M.A.),
Books by. Dy. 8vo, c., 7s. 6d. net each.

Notes on the Science of Picture-making. With Photogravure Frontis.

Notes on the Art of Rembrandt. With Frontispiece and 44 Plates.

HOME OF TO-DAY (The)—By a Woman Who Keeps One. Crown 8vo, cloth, 5s. net.

HOOD'S (THOMAS) Choice Works in Prose and Verse. With Life of the Author, Portrait, and 200 Illusts. Crown 8vo, cloth, 3s. 6d. net.

HOOK'S (THEODORE) Choice Humorous Works. With Life and Frontispiece. Cr. 8vo, cloth, 3s. 6d. net.

HORNIMAN (ROY), Novels by.
Bellamy the Magnificent. Crown 8vo, cloth, 6s. net and 2s. net.
Lord Cammarleigh's Secret. Crown 8vo, cloth, 3s. 6d. net.
Israel Rank. Cr. 8vo, cloth, 3s. 6d. net.

HORNUNG (E. W.), Novels by.
Crown 8vo, cloth, 3s. 6d. net each.

Stingaree. | A Thief in the Night.
The Shadow of the Rope. Also at 2s. net.

HOUGHTON (MARY). — In the Enemy's Country. Foreword by ED-WARD GARNETT. Cr. 8vo, cloth, 5s. net.

HUEFFER (FORD MADOX), Novels by.
A Call: The Tale of Two Passions. Crown 8vo, cloth, 3s. 6d. net.
The Young Lovell. Cr. 8vo, cloth, 6s. net.

HUGO (VICTOR). — The Outlaw of Iceland. Translated by Sir GILBERT CAMPBELL. Crown 8vo, cl., 3s. 6d. net.

HULL (ELEANOR), Selected and Annotated by. — The Poem-book of the Gael. Small cr. 8vo, cloth, 6s. net.

HUME (FERGUS), Novels by.

The Lady From Nowhere. Cr. 8vo, cloth, 3s. 6d. net.

The Millionaire Mystery. Crown 8vo, cloth, 3s. 6d. net.

The Wheeling Light. Crown 8vo, cloth, 3s. 6d. net.

HUNGERFORD (Mrs.), Novels by. Cr. 8vo, cl., 3s. 6d. net each.

The Professor's Experiment.
Lady Verner's Flight.
Lady Patty.
Peter's Wife.
The Red-House Mystery.
An Unsatisfactory Lover.
A Maiden All Forlorn.
A Mental Struggle.
Marvel.
A Modern Circe.
In Durance Vile.
April's Lady.
The Three Graces.
Nora Creina.
An Anxious Moment.
A Point of Conscience.
The Coming of Chloe.
Lovice.

POPULAR EDITIONS, med. 8vo, 9d. net each.
The Red-House Mystery.
A Modern Circe.

HUNT (Mrs. ALFRED) and VIOLET HUNT. — The Governess. Cr. 8vo, cl., 6s. net.

HYAMSON (ALBERT). — A History of the Jews in England. With 18 Illusts. Demy 8vo, cloth, 4s. 6d. net.

HYATT (A. H.), Topographical Anthologies compiled by. Crown 8vo, cloth, full gilt side, gilt top, 5s. net each. Also, FINE-PAPER EDITIONS, without Illustrations, Pott 8vo, cloth, 2s. 6d. net each; leather, gilt top, 4s. net each.

The Charm of Venice: an Anthology. With 12 Ill. in Colour by HARALD SUND.

The Charm of London. With 12 Illusts. in Colour by YOSHIO MARKINO.

The Charm of Paris. With 12 Illustrations in Colour by HARRY MORLEY.

The Charm of Edinburgh. With 12 Illusts. in Colour by HARRY MORLEY.

INCE (MABEL), Novels by.

Each with Frontispiece, cr. 8vo, cl., 6s. net each.

The Wisdom of Waiting.
The Commonplace & Clementine.

14

INCHBOLD (A. C.), Novels by.
The Road of No Return. Cr. 8vo cloth, 3s. 6d. net.

Love in a Thirsty Land. Cr. 8vo, cloth, 6s. net.

INDUSTRIAL OUTLOOK (The). —By Various Authors. Edited by H SANDERSON FURNISS. Crown 8vo, cloth, 3s. 6d. net.

INTERNATIONAL CARTOONS OF THE WAR. Selected by H. PEARL ADAM. Demy 4to, cloth, 3s. 6d. net.

IONIDES (CYRIL). — *See under* ATKINS (J. B), p. 2.

IRVING (WASHINGTON).—Old **Christmas.** Square 16mo, cl., 1s. net.

JAMES (G. W.). — Scraggles : **The Story of a Sparrow.** Illust. Cr. 8vo, cloth, 2s. 6d. net.

JAMES (HENRY), Pictures and other Passages from. Selected by RUTH HEAD. Post 8vo, bds., 3s. 6d. net.

"JASON"—Past and Future. Crown 8vo, cloth, 3s. 6d. net.

JEFFERIES (RICHARD), by.

The Pageant of Summer. Long fcap. decorated cover, 1s. net.

The Life of the Fields. Post 8vo, cl., 2s. 6d. net ; LARGE TYPE, FINE PAPER EDITION, pott 8vo, cloth, 2s. 6d. net ; leather, gilt top, 4s. net. *Also* a NEW EDITION, with 12 Illustrations in Colours by M. U. CLARKE, cr. 8vo, cl., 5s. net.

The Open Air. Post 8vo, cl., 2s. 6d. net. LARGE TYPE, FINE PAPER EDITION, pott 8vo, cloth, 2s. 6d. net ; leather, gilt top, 4s. net. *Also* a NEW EDITION. Illustrated. Uniform with above.

Nature near London. Crown 8vo, buckram, 5s. net ; post 8vo, cl., 2s. 6d. net ; LARGE TYPE, FINE PAPER EDITION, pott 8vo, cloth, 2s. 6d. net ; leather, gilt top, 4s. net. *Also* a NEW EDITION. Illustrated. Uniform with above.

The Pocket Richard Jefferies: Passages chosen by A. H. HYATT. 16mo, cloth, 2s. 6d. net ; leather, gilt top, 4s. net.

JENKINS (HESTER D.).—Be- hind Turkish Lattices. With 24 Illustrations. Crown 8vo, cloth, 6s. net.

JERROLD (TOM), Books by. Post 8vo, cl., 1s. 6d. net each.

The Garden that Paid the Rent. **Household Horticulture.**

Our War-Time Kitchen Garden : The Plants We Grow, and How We Cook Them. Post 8vo, cloth, 1s. net.

JOFFRE (General).—My March to Timbuctoo. With a Character Sketch by ERNEST DIMNET. Cr. 8vo, cloth, 2s. net.

JOHNSTONE (Arthur).—Recol- lections of R. L. Stevenson in the Pacific. With Portrait and Facsimile Letter. Crown 8vo, buckram, 6s. net.

JONES (CECIL DUNCAN).— **The Everlasting Search :** A Ro-mance. Crown 8vo, cloth, 6s. net.

JONSON'S (BEN) Works. With Notes, etc., by WILLIAM GIFFORD, Edited by Colonel CUNNINGH . Three Vols., crown 8vo, cloth, 3s. 6d. net each.

JOSEPHUS, The Complete Works of. Translated by WILLIAM WHISTON. Illustrated. Two Vols., demy 8vo, cloth, 5s. net each.

KEATS (JOHN), The Poems of. *See* FLORENCE PRESS BOOKS, page 10.

KEMPLING (W. BAILEY-).—The Poets Royal of England and Scot-land. With 6 Portraits. Small 8vo, parchment, 6s. net ; vellum, 7s. 6d. net. (See also KING'S CLASSICS, p. 16.)

KENT (Lieut.-Comm.). — Poor Dear Providence: A Naval Love Story. Crown 8vo, cloth, 6s. net.

KEYNES (HELEN MARY), Novels by. Crown 8vo, cloth, 6s. net. each.

The Spanish Marriage. **Honour the King.**

KING (LEONARD W., M.A.).—

A History of Babylonia and Assyria from Prehistoric Times to the Persian Conquest. With Plans and Illustrations. 3 vols. royal 8vo, cloth. Each vol. separately, 18s. net ; or the 3 vols. if ordered at one time, £2 10s. net.

Vol. I.—**A History of Sumer and Akkad:** An account of the Early Races of Babylonia from Prehistoric Times to the Foundation of the Babylonian Monarchy.

„ II.—**A History of Babylon** from the Foundation of the Monarchy, about B.C. 2000, until the Conquest of Babylon by Cyrus, B.C. 539.

„ III.—**A History of Assyria** from the Earliest Period until the Fall of Nineveh. B.C. 606. [Preparing.

KING'S CLASSICS (The).

Under the General Editorship of Prof. ISRAEL GOLLANCZ, D.Litt. Post 8vo, quarter - bound antique grey boards or red cloth, 2s. 6d. net : Double Vols., 3s. 6d. net. Quarter vellum, grey cl. sides, 3s. 6d. net : Double Vols., 5s. net. Three-quarter vellum, Oxford side-papers, gilt top, 5s. net : Double Vols., 7s. 6d. net. † signifies Double Volumes. * can be supplied for School use in wrappers at 1s. net each.

1. **The Love of Books: the Philobiblon of Richard de Bury.** Trans. by E. C THOMAS.
†2. **Six Dramas of Calderon.** Trans by ED FITZGERALD. Edited by H. OELSNER, M.A
3. **The Chronicle of Jocelin of Brakelond.** Trans. from the Latin, with Notes, by L. C. JANE, M.A. Introd. by ABBOT GASQUET.
4. **Life of Sir Thomas More.** By WILLIAM ROPER. With Letters to and from his Daughter.
5. **Eikon Basilike.** Ed. by ED ALMACK, F.S.A.
6. **Kings' Letters.** Part I.: From Alfred to the Coming of the Tudors. Edited by ROBERT STEELE.
7. **Kings' Letters. Part II.:** From the Early Tudors ; with Letters of Henry VIII. and Anne Boleyn.
8. **Chaucer's Knight's Tale.** In modern English by Prof. SKEAT.
*9. **Chaucer's Man o' Law's Tale, Squire's Tale, and Nun's Priest's Tale.** In modern English by Prof. SKEAT.
*10. **Chaucer's Prioress's Tale, Pardoner's Tale, Clerk's Tale, and Canon's Yeoman's Tale.** In modern English by Prof. SKEAT. (See also Nos. 9, 47, 48.)
11. **The Romance of Fulk Fitzwarine.** Translated by ALICE KEMP - WELCH ; Introduction by Prof. BRANDIN.
12. **The Story of Cupid and Psyche.** From "The Golden Ass," ADLINGTON'S Translation. Edited by W. H. D. ROUSE.
13. **Life of Margaret Godolphin.** By JOHN EVELYN.
14. **Early Lives of Dante.** Translated by Rev. P. H. WICKSTEED.
15. **The Falstaff Letters.** By JAMES WHITE.
16. **Polonius.** By EDWARD FITZGERALD.
17. **Mediæval Lore.** From BARTHOLOMÆUS ANGLICUS. Edited by ROBERT STEELE. With Preface by WILLIAM MORRIS.
18. **The Vision of Piers the Plowman.** By WILLIAM LANGLAND. In modern English by Prof. SKEAT.
19. **The Gull's Hornbook.** By THOMAS DEKKER. Edited by R. B. McKERROW, M.A.
†20. **The Nun's Rule, or Ancren Riwle in modern English.** Edited by ABBOT GASQUET.
21. **Memoirs of Robert Cary, Earl of Monmouth.** Edited by G. H. POWELL.
22. **Early Lives of Charlemagne.** Translated by A. J. GRANT. (See also No. 45.)

KING'S CLASSICS—continued.

23. **Cicero's "Friendship," "Old Age," and "Scipio's Dream."** Edited by W. H. D. ROUSE, Litt.D.
†24. **Wordsworth's Prelude.** With Notes by W. B. WORSFOLD, M.A.
25. **The Defence of Guenevere, and other Poems by William Morris.** With Introduction by ROBERT STEELE.
26, 27. **Browning's Men and Women.** Notes by W. B. WORSFOLD, M.A. [In 2 Vols.
28. **Poe's Poems.** Notes by EDWARD HUTTON.
29. **Shakespeare's Sonnets.** Edited by C. C. STOPES.
30. **George Eliot's Silas Marner.** With Introduction by Dr. R. GARNETT.
31. **Goldsmith's Vicar of Wakefield.** With Introduction by Dr. R. GARNETT.
32. **Charles Reade's Peg Woffington.** With Introduction by Dr. R. GARNETT.
33. **The Household of Sir Thomas More.** By ANNE MANNING. With Preface by Dr. R. GARNETT. (See also Nos. 4, 40.)
34. **Sappho: One Hundred Lyrics.** By BLISS CARMAN.
35. **Wine, Women, and Song: Mediæval Latin Students' Songs.** Translated with Introd., by J. ADDINGTON SYMONDS.
36, 37. **George Pettie's Petite Pallace of Pettie His Pleasure.** Edited by Prof. I. GOLLANCZ. [In Two Volumes.
38. **Walpole's Castle of Otranto.** With Preface by Miss SPURGEON.
39. **The Poets Royal of England and Scotland.** Original Poems by Royal and Noble Persons. Edited by W. BAILEY KEMPLING.
40. **Sir Thomas More's Utopia.** Edited by ROBERT STEELE, F.S.A.
*41. **Chaucer's Legend of Good Women.** In modern English by Prof. SKEAT.
42. **Swift's Battle of the Books, &c.** Edited by A. GUTHKELCH.
43. **Sir William Temple upon the Gardens of Epicurus, with other XVIIth Century Essays.** Edited by A. FORBES SIEVEKING, F.S.A.
45. **The Song of Roland.** Translated by Mrs. CROSLAND. With Introduction by Prof. BRANDIN. (See also No. 22.)
46. **Dante's Vita Nuova.** The Italian text, with ROSSETTI'S translation, and Introd. by Dr. H. OELSNER. (See also No. 14.)
47. **Chaucer's Prologue and Minor Poems.** In modern English by Prof. SKEAT.
*48. **Chaucer's Parliament of Birds and House of Fame.** In modern English by Prof. SKEAT.
49. **Mrs. Gaskell's Cranford.** With Introduction by R. BRIMLEY JOHNSON.
50. **Pearl.** An English Poem of the Fourteenth Century. Edited, with Modern Rendering, by Prof. I. GOLLANCZ. [Preparing.
51, 52. **Kings' Letters. Parts III. and IV.** Edited by ROBERT STEELE, F.S.A. [In Two Volumes. Preparing.
53. **The English Correspondence of Saint Boniface.** Trans. by EDWARD KYLIE, M.A.
56. **The Cavalier to His Lady:** XVIIth Century Love Songs. Edited by FRANK SIDGWICK.
57. **Asser's Life of King Alfred.** Translated by L. C. JANE, M.A.
58. **Translations from the Icelandic.** Translated by Rev W. C. GREEN, M.A.
59. **The Rule of St Benedict.** Translated by ABBOT GASQUET.
60. **Daniel's "Delia" and Drayton's "Idea."** Ed. by ARUNDELL ESDAILE, M.A.
61. **The Book of the Duke of True Lovers.** Translated from CHRISTINE DE PISAN by ALICE KEMP-WELCH.
62. **Of the Tumbler of Our Lady, and other Miracles.** Translated from GAUTIER DE COINCI, &c., by ALICE KEMP-WELCH.
63. **The Chatelaine of Vergi.** Translated by ALICE KEMP-WELCH. With Introduction by L. BRANDIN, Ph.D.

KRYSHANOVSKAYA, (V. I.) —
The Torch-Bearers of Bohemia. Translated from the Russian by J. M. SOSKICE. Crown 8vo, cloth, 5s. net.

LAMB'S (CHARLES) Collected
Works in Prose and Verse, including 'Poetry for Children' and 'Prince Dorus.' Edited by R. H. SHEPHERD. Crown 8vo, cloth, 3s. 6d. net.

The Essays of Elia. (Both Series.) FINE PAPER EDITION, pott 8vo, cloth, 2s. 6d. net; leather, gilt top, 4s. net.

LANE (EDWARD WILLIAM).
The Arabian Nights. Illustrated by W. HARVEY. With Preface by STANLEY LANE-POOLE. 3 Vols., demy 8vo, cloth, 5s. net each.

LASAR (CHARLES A.).—Prac-
tical Hints for Art Students. Illustrated. Post 8vo, cloth, 3s. 6d. net.

LAURISTOUN (PETER). — The
Painted Mountain. Cr. 8vo, cloth, 6s. net.

LAWRENCE (D. H.).—Look !
We have come Through ! Small fcap. 4to. boards, 5s. net.

LEE (VERNON).—The Ballet of
the Nations: A Present-day Morality. Decorated by MAXWELL ARMFIELD. Demy 4to, boards, 3s. 6d. net.

LEITH (MRS. DISNEY).—The
Boyhood of Algernon Charles
Swinburne. With Extracts
from Private Letters. Illustrated. Crown 8vo, cloth, 6s. net. See also under Swinburne, p. 30.

LELAND (C. G.).—A Manual of
Mending and Repairing. With Diagrams. Crown 8vo, cloth, 5s. net.

LEPELLETIER (EDMOND). —
Madame Sans-Gêne. Translated by JOHN DE VILLIERS. Post 8vo. cloth, 3s. 6d. net; POPULAR EDITION, medium 8vo, 9d. net.

LITTLE (MAUDE), Novels by.
Crown 8vo, cloth, 6s. net each.
At the Sign of the Burning Bush.
A Woman on the Threshold.
The Children's Bread.

LLOYD (Theodosia).—Innocence
in the Wilderness. Cr. 8vo, cloth, 6s. net.

LINTON (E. LYNN), Works by.
Crown 8vo. cloth, 3s. 6d. net each.
Patricia Kemball. | Ione.
The Atonement of Leam Dundas.
The World Well Lost. 12 Illusts.
The One Too Many.
Under which Lord ? With 12 Illusts.
'My Love.' | Sowing the Wind.
Paston Carew. | Dulcie Everton.
With a Silken Thread.
The Rebel of the Family.
An Octave of Friends.

Patricia Kemball. POPULAR EDITION, medium 8vo, 9d. net.

LUCAS (E. V.), Books by.
Anne's Terrible Good Nature, and other Stories for Children. With 12 Illustrations. Crown 8vo, cloth, 6s. net.

A Book of Verses for Children. Crown 8vo, cloth, 5s. net.

Three Hundred Games and Pastimes. By E. V. LUCAS and ELIZABETH LUCAS. Pott 4to. cloth, 6s. net.

The Flamp, and other Stories. Royal 16mo, cloth, 1s. net.

LYRE D'AMOUR (La).—An An-
thology of French Love Poems. Selected, with Introduction and Notes, by C. B. LEWIS. Cr. 8vo, cloth, 5s. net.

MACNAIR (WILSON). — Glass
Houses. Crown 8vo, cloth, 6s. net.

McCARTHY (JUSTIN), Books by.
A History of the Four Georges
and of William the Fourth. Four Vols., demy 8vo, cl., 10s. 6d. net ea.

A History of Our Own Times from the Accession of Queen Victoria to the General Election of 1880. LIBRARY EDITION. Four Vols., demy 8vo, cloth, 10s. 6d. net each.—Also the POPULAR EDITION, in Four Vols., crown 8vo, cloth, 5s. net each.—And the JUBILEE EDITION, with an Appendix of Events to the end of 1886, in 2 Vols., large post 8vo, cloth, 10s. 6d. net.

A History of Our Own Times, Vol. V., from 1880 to the Diamond Jubilee. Demy 8vo, cloth, 10s. 6d. net ; crown 8vo, cloth, 5s. net.

A History of Our Own Times, Vols. VI. and VII., from 1897 to Accession of Edward VII. 2 Vols., demy 8vo, cloth, 21s. net ; crown 8vo, cloth, 5s. net each.

A Short History of Our Own Times, from the Accession of Queen Victoria to the Accession of King Edward VII. Crown 8vo, cloth, gilt top, 5s. net ; also the POPULAR EDITION, post 8vo, cl., 2s. 6d. net ; and the CHEAP EDITION (to the year 1880), med. 8vo, 9d. net.

McCARTHY (JUSTIN).—*continued.*
Our Book of Memories. Letters from JUSTIN McCARTHY to Mrs. CAMPBELL PRAED. With Portraits and Views. Demy 8vo, cloth, 12s. 6d. net.

FINE PAPER EDITIONS.

Pott 8vo, cloth, 2s. 6d. net per vol.; leather, gilt top, 4s. net per vol.

The Reign of Queen Anne, in 1 Vol.
A History of the Four Georges and of William IV., in 2 vols.
A History of Our Own Times from Accession of Q. Victoria to 1901, in 4 Vols.

Crown 8vo, cloth, 3s. 6d. net each.

The Waterdale Neighbours.
My Enemy's Daughter.
A Fair Saxon. | Linley Rochford.
Dear Lady Disdain. | The Dictator.
Miss Misanthrope. With 12 Illusts.
Donna Quixote. With 12 Illustrations.
The Comet of a Season.
Maid of Athens. With 12 Illustrations.
Camiola.
Red Diamonds. | The Riddle Ring.
The Three Disgraces.
Mononia.
Julian Revelstone.

'The Right Honourable.' By JUSTIN McCARTHY and Mrs. CAMPBELL PRAED. Crown 8vo, cloth, 6s. net.

MacCARTHY (MARY).—A Pier and a Band. Crown 8vo, cloth, 6s. net.

McCARTHY (J. H.), Works by.
The French Revolution. (Constituent Assembly, 1789-91.) Four Vols., demy 8vo, cloth, 10s. 6d. net each.
An Outline of the History of Ireland. Crown 8vo, 1s. net; cloth, 1s. 6d. net.
Our Sensation Novel. Crown 8vo, 1s. net; cloth, 1s. 6d. net.
Doom: An Atlantic Episode. Cr. 8vo, 1s.net.
Lily Lass. Cr. 8vo, 1s. net; cl., 1s. 6d. net.
A London Legend. Cr. 8vo, cloth, 3s. 6d. net.

MACAULAY (LORD).—The History of England. LARGE TYPE, FINE PAPER EDITION, in 5 vols. pott 8vo, cloth, 2s. 6d. net per vol.; leather, gilt top, 4s. net per vol.

McCURDY (EDWARD).—Essays in Fresco. With 6 Illustrations. Crown 8vo, buckram, 5s. net.

MACDONALD (Dr. GEORGE), Books by.

Works of Fancy and Imagination Ten Vols., 16mo, Grolier cloth, 2s. 6d. net each. Also in 16mo, cloth, 2s. 6d. net per Vol.; leather, gilt top, 4s. net per Vol.

Vol.	
„	I. WITHIN AND WITHOUT — THE HIDDEN LIFE.
„	II. THE DISCIPLE — THE GOSPEL WOMEN—BOOK OF SONNETS—ORGAN SONGS.
„	III. VIOLIN SONGS—SONGS OF THE DAYS AND NIGHTS—A BOOK OF DREAMS—ROADSIDE POEMS —POEMS FOR CHILDREN.
„	IV. PARABLES — BALLADS — SCOTCH
„	V. & VI. PHANTASTES. [SONGS.
„	VII. THE PORTENT.
„	VIII. THE LIGHT PRINCESS — THE GIANT'S HEART—SHADOWS.
„	IX. CROSS PURPOSES—GOLDEN KEY CARASOYN—LITTLE DAYLIGHT.
„	X. THE CRUEL PAINTER—THE WOW O'RIVVEN—THE CASTLE—THE BROKEN SWORDS—THE GRAY WOLF—UNCLE CORNELIUS.

Poetical Works. 2 Vols., cr. 8vo, buckram, 12s. net; pott 8vo, cl., 2s. 6d. net per vol.; leather, gilt top, 4s. net per vol.
Heather and Snow. Crown 8vo, cloth, 3s. 6d. net.
Lilith. Crown 8vo, cloth, 6s. net.

The Pocket George MacDonald: Passages Chosen by A. H. HYATT. 16mo, cloth, 2s. 6d. net; leather, gilt top, 4s. net.

MACHRAY (ROBERT), Novels by. Crown 8vo, cloth, 3s. 6d. net each.
A Blow over the Heart.
The Private Detective.
Sentenced to Death.
The Mystery of Lincoln's Inn.
Her Honour.

The Woman Wins. Cr. 8vo, cloth, 6s. net.

MACKAY (WILLIAM). — A Mender of Nets. Crown 8vo, cloth, 6s. net.

McLEOD (IRENE RUTHERFORD).—Songs to Save a Soul. Pott 8vo, cloth, 2s. 6d. net; parchment gilt, 3s. 6d. net.
Swords for Life. Pott 8vo, cl. 2s. 6d.net.
One Mother (Reprinted from above). Cr. 8vo, paper. with photogravure, 6d. net.

MAGNA CHARTA: A Facsimile of Original, in Gold and Colours, 3s. 6d. net.

MALLOCK (W. H.), Works by.
The New Republic. FINE PAPER EDITION, pott 8vo, cloth, 2s. 6d. net; leather, gilt top, 4s. net.

MALLOCK (W. H.).—*continued.*
Is Life Worth Living? Cr. 8vo, 5s. net.

MALLORY (Sir THOMAS).—
Mort d'Arthur, Selections from, edited by B. M. RANKING. Post 8vo, cl., 2s. net

MARGUERITTE (PAUL and VICTOR), Novels by.
The Disaster. Translated by F. LEES. Crown 8vo, cloth, 3s. 6d. net. WAR EDITION, cloth, 2s. net.
Vanity. Translated by K. S. WEST. Crown 8vo, cl., Portrait-Frontispiece, 3s. 6d. net.

MARKINO (Yoshio), Books by.
A Japanese Artist in London. By YOSHIO MARKINO. With 8 Illusts. in Three Colours and 4 in Monochrome by the Author. Cr. 8vo, cloth, 6s. net.
My Recollections and Reflections. by YOSHIO MARKINO. With 9 Illusts. in Colour and 6 in Sepia by the Author. Crown 8vo, cloth, 6s. net.
The Charm of London. Passages selected by A. H. HYATT. With 12 Illusts. in Colour by YOSHIO MARKINO. Cr. 8vo, cloth gilt, 5s. net.
Oxford from Within. By HUGH DE SÉLINCOURT. With a Note and 12 Illusts. in Three Colours and 8 in Sepia by YOSHIO MARKINO. Demy 8vo, cl., 5s. net. Large fcap. 4to, cloth, 10s. 6d. net.
The Colour of London. By W. J. LOFTIE, F.S.A. With Introduction by M. H. SPIELMANN, Preface and 48 Illustrations in Colour and 12 in Sepia by YOSHIO MARKINO.
The Colour of Paris. By MM. LES ACADÉMICIENS GONCOURT. With Introduction by L. BÉNÉDITE, Preface and 48 Illustrations in Colour and 12 in Sepia by YOSHIO MARKINO.
The Colour of Rome. By OLAVE M. POTTER. With Introduction by DOUGLAS SLADEN, Preface and 48 Illustrations in Colour and 12 in Sepia by YOSHIO MARKINO.
London: Pictured by YOSHIO MARKINO. 16 Coloured Plates, with Literary Extracts. Large fcap. 4to, boards, 1s. 6d. net.

Crown 8vo, cloth, 6s. net.
The Story of Yone Noguchi. By Himself. With 8 Illusts. by YOSHIO MARKINO.

MARLOWE'S Works, including his Translations. Edited with Notes by Col. CUNNINGHAM. Cr. 8vo, cl., 3s. 6d. net.

MARSH (RICHARD), Novels by.
A Spoiler of Men. Cr. 8vo, cl., 3s. 6d. net; POPULAR EDITION, med. 8vo, 9d. net.

Crown 8vo, cloth.
Justice—Suspended. 3s. 6d. net.
Margot—and her Judges. 6s. net.
His Love or His Life. 6s. net.

MARSHALL (RACHEL).—A Ride on a Rocking Horse. Illustrated in Colour by the Author. Fcap. 4to, boards, 3s. 6d. net.

MASSINGER'S Plays. From the Text of WILLIAM GIFFORD. Edited by Col. CUNNINGHAM. Cr. 8vo, cl., 3s. 6d. net.

MASTER OF GAME (THE): The Oldest English Book on Hunting. By EDWARD, Second Duke of York. Edited by W. A. and F. BAILLIE-GROHMAN. With Introduction by THEODORE ROOSEVELT. Photogravure Frontis. and 23 Illustns. Large cr. 8vo. cl., 7s. 6d. net; parchment, 10s. 6d. net.

MAX O'RELL, Books by.
Crown 8vo, cloth, 3s. 6d. net each.
Her Royal Highness Woman.
Between Ourselves.
Rambles in Womanland.

H.R.H. Woman, POPULAR EDITION, medium 8vo, 9d. net.

MAYNE (ETHEL COLBURN).—
Browning's Heroines. With Frontispiece and Title in Colour and other Decorations by MAXWELL ARMFIELD. Large crown 8vo, cloth, 6s. net.

MEADE (L. T.), Novels by.
Crown 8vo, cloth, 3s. 6d. net each.
A Soldier of Fortune.
In an Iron Grip. | The Siren.
Dr. Rumsey's Patient.
On the Brink of a Chasm.
The Way of a Woman.
A Son of Ishmael.
An Adventuress.
The Blue Diamond.
A Stumble by the Way.
This Troublesome World.

MEDIEVAL LIBRARY (The New). Small crown 8vo, pure rag paper, boards, 5s. net per vol.; pigskin with clasps, 7s. 6d. net per vol.
1. **The Book of the Duke of True Lovers.** Translated from the Middle French of CHRISTINE DE PISAN, with Notes by ALICE KEMP-WELCH. Woodcut Title and 6 Photogravures.
2. **Of the Tumbler of our Lady, and other Miracles.** Translated from the Middle French of GAUTIER DE COINCI, &c., with Notes by ALICE KEMP-WELCH. Woodcut and 7 Photogravures.
3. **The Chatelaine of Vergi.** Translated from the Middle French by ALICE KEMP-WELCH, with the original Text, and an Introduction by Dr. L. BRANDIN. Woodcut Title and 5 Photogravures.
4. **The Babees' Book.** Edited, with Notes, by EDITH RICKERT. Woodcut Title and 6 Photogravures.
5. **The Book of the Divine Consolation of Saint Angela da Foligno.** Translated by MARY G. STEEGMANN. Woodcut Title and Illusts. Small crown 8vo, pure rag paper, boards, 5s. net per vol.; pigskin with clasps, 7s. 6d. net per vol.

MEDIEVAL LIBRARY (The New)—*cont*

6. **The Legend of the Holy Fina, Virgin of Santo Geminiano.** Translated by M. MANSFIELD. Woodcut Title and 6 Photogravures.

7. **Early English Romances of Love.** Edited in Modern English by EDITH RICKERT. 5 Photogravures.

8. **Early English Romances of Friendship.** Edited, with Notes, by EDITH RICKERT. 6 Photogravures.

9. **The Cell of Self-Knowledge.** Seven Early Mystical Treatises printed in 1851. Edited, with Introduction and Notes, by EDMUND GARDNER, M.A. Collotype Frontispiece in two colours.

10. **Ancient English Christmas Carols, 1400-1700.** Collected and arranged by EDITH RICKERT. With 8 Photogravures. Special price of this volume, boards, 7s. 6d. net; pigskin with clasps, 10s. 6d. net.

11. **Trobador Poets:** Selections. Translated from the Provençal, with Introduction and Notes, by BARBARA SMYTHE. With Coloured Frontispiece and Decorative Initials.

12. **Cligés:** A Romance. Translated with an Introduction by L. J. GARDINER, M.A.Lond., from the Old French of CHRÉTIEN DE TROYES. With a Frontisp.

MÉRAL (PAUL).—The Book of Recitatives. Translated from the French by LADY ROTHERMERE. 188 copies printed on hand-made paper. Demy 4to, £2 2s. net. Also 12 copies printed on vellum and signed by the Author, £6 6s. net.

MERRICK (LEONARD), by.
Crown 8vo, cloth, 3s. 6d. net each.
The Man who was Good.
This Stage of Fools.
Cynthia.

METHVEN (PAUL), Novels by.
Crown 8vo, cloth, 6s. net. each.
Influences.
Billy.

MEYNELL (ALICE).—The Flower of the Mind: a Choice among the Best Poems. In 16mo, cloth, 2s. 6d. net; leather, gilt top, 4s. net.

MITCHELL (EDM.), Novels by.
Crown 8vo, cloth, 3s. 6d. net each.
The Lone Star Rush. With 8 Illusts.
The Belforts of Culben.
Only a Nigger.

MITFORD (BERTRAM), Novels by. Crown 8vo, cloth, 3s. 6d. net each.
Renshaw Fanning's Quest.
Triumph of Hilary Blachland.
Haviland's Chum.
Harley Greenoak's Charge.
The Gun-Runner.
The Luck of Gerard Ridgeley.
The King's Assegai. With 6 Illusts.

POPULAR EDITIONS, med. 8vo, 9d. net each.
The Gun-Runner.
The Luck of Gerard Ridgeley.

MOLESWORTH (Mrs.).—Hathercourt Rectory. Crown 8vo, cloth, 3s. 6d. net.

MONCRIEFF (W. D. SCOTT-).—The Abdication: A Drama. With 7 Etchings. Imp. 4to, buckram, 21s. net.

MORROW (W. C.).—Bohemian Paris of To-Day. With 106 Illusts. by EDOUARD CUCUEL. Small demy 8vo, cloth, 5s. net

MOZART'S OPERAS: a Critical Study. By E. J DENT. Illustrated. Demy 8vo, cloth, 12s. 6d. net.

MUDDOCK (J. E.), Stories by. Crown 8vo, cloth, 3s. 6d. net each.
Basile the Jester.
The Golden Idol.

MURRAY (D. CHRISTIE), Novels by. Crown 8vo, cl., 3s. 6d. net each.
A Life's Atonement.
Joseph's Coat. With 12 Illustrations.
Coals of Fire. With 3 Illustrations.
Val Strange. | A Wasted Crime
A Capful o' Nails. | Hearts.
The Way of the World.
Mount Despair. | A Model Father.
Old Blazer's Hero.
By the Gate of the Sea.
A Bit of Human Nature.
First Person Singular.
Bob Martin's Little Girl.
Time's Revenges.
Cynic Fortune. | In Direst Peril.
This Little World.
A Race for Millions.
The Church of Humanity.
Tales in Prose and Verse.
Despair's Last Journey.
V.C. | Verona's Father.
His Own Ghost.

Joseph's Coat. POPULAR EDITION, 9d. net.

MURRAY (D. CHRISTIE) and
HENRY HERMAN, Novels by.
Crown 8vo, cloth, 3s. 6d. net each.
One Traveller Returns.
The Bishops' Bible.
Paul Jones's Alias. With Illustrations.

NEVILL (RALPH).
The Man of Pleasure. With 28
Illustrations, Coloured and plain. Demy
8vo, cloth, 12s. 6d. net.

NEWBOLT (HENRY). — Taken
from the Enemy. With 8 Coloured
Illusts. by GERALD LEAKE. Cr. 8vo, cl.,
3s. 6d. net and 2s. net.

NICHOLS (ROBERT).—Ardours
and Endurances. Crown 8vo,
cloth, 3s. 6d. net.
The Assault, and other War
Poems from 'Ardours and
Endurances.' Crown 8vo, paper
with cover design by C. R. W. NEVINSON.
1s. 3d. net.

NIJINSKY, THE ART OF. By
GEOFFREY WHITWORTH. Illustrated in
Colour by DOROTHY MULLOCK. Post
8vo, cloth, 3s. 6d. net.

NISBET (HUME). — 'Bail Up!'
Crown 8vo, cloth, 3s. 6d. net; medium
8vo, 9d. net.

NOGUCHI (YONE), The Story of.
Told by Himself. With 8 Illustrations
by YOSHIO MARKINO. Cr. 8vo, cl., 6s. net.

NORRIS (W. E.), Novels by.
Crown 8vo, cloth, 3s. 6d. net each.
Saint Ann's. | **Billy Bellew.**
Miss Wentworth's Idea.

OHNET (GEORGES), Novels by.
Crown 8vo, cloth, 3s. 6d. net each.
A Weird Gift.
The Path of Glory.
Love's Depths.
The Money-maker.
The Woman of Mystery.
The Conqueress.

OLIPHANT (Mrs.), Novels by.
Cr. 8vo, cloth, 3s. 6d. net.
The Primrose Path.
The Greatest Heiress in England
Whiteladies.
The Sorceress.

OLYMPIA : the Latin Text of
Boccaccio's Fourteenth Eclogue,
with an English rendering and other
Supplementary Matter by ISRAEL GOL-
LANCZ, Litt.D., and Photogravure Frontispiece. Printed in the Florence Press
Type upon hand-made paper. Edition
limited to 500 copies. Fcap. 4to, boards,
6s. net ; vellum, 12s. 6d. net.

O'SHAUGHNESSY (ARTHUR).
Music & Moonlight. Fcp. 8vo, cloth,
6s. net.

OUIDA, Novels by. Crown 8vo,
cloth, 3s. 6d. net each.

Tricotrin.	**A Dog of Flanders.**
Ruffino.	**Cecil Castlemaine's**
Othmar.	**Gage.**
Frescoes.	**Princess Napraxine.**
Wanda.	**Held in Bondage.**
Ariadne.	**Under Two Flags.**
Pascarel.	**Folle-Farine.** [**Shoes.**
Chandos.	**Two Little Wooden**
Moths.	**A Village Commune.**
Puck.	**In a Winter City.**
Idalia.	**Santa Barbara.**
Bimbi.	**In Maremma.**
Signa.	**Strathmore.**
Friendship.	**Pipistrello.**
Guilderoy.	**Two Offenders.**
	Syrlin.

A Rainy June. | **The Massarenes.**
The Waters of Edera.

POPULAR EDITIONS, medium 8vo,
9d. net each.

Under Two Flags.	**Moths.**
Held in Bondage.	**Puck.**
Strathmore.	**Tricotrin.**
The Massarenes.	**Chandos.**
Friendship.	**Ariadne.**

Two Little Wooden Shoes.
Idalia. | **Othmar.** | **Pascarel.**
Folle-Farine. | **Princess Napraxine**
Wanda. | **In Maremma.**

Two Little Wooden Shoes. LARGE
TYPE EDITION. Fcap. 8vo, cloth, 1s. net.

Wisdom, Wit, and Pathos, selected
from the Works of OUIDA by F. SYDNEY
MORRIS. Pott 8vo, cloth, 2s. 6d. net ;
leather, gilt top, 4s. net.

OXFORD FROM WITHIN. By
HUGH DE SÉLINCOURT. With a Note and
12 Illustrations in Colour and 8 in Sepia
by YOSHIO MARKINO. Demy 8vo, cloth,
5s. net.

PAIN (BARRY).—Eliza's Husband. Fcap. 8vo, 1s. net; cl., 1s. 6d. net.

PANDURANG HARI; or, Memoirs of a Hindoo. Post 8vo, cloth, 3s. 6d. net.

PARIS.—Bohemian Paris of To-day. By W. C. MORROW. With 106 Illustrations by E. CUCUEL. Small demy 8vo, cloth, 5s. net.

The Illustrated Catalogue of the Paris Salon. With about 300 illusts. Published annually to 1914. Demy 8vo, 3s. net.

See also under Markino (Yoshio), p. 19.

PATTERSON (MARJORIE).— The Dust of the Road: A Novel. Crown 8vo, cloth, 6s. net.

PAYN (JAMES), Novels by.

Crown 8vo, cloth, 3s. 6d. net each.

Lost Sir Massingberd.
The Clyffards of Clyffe.
A County Family.
Less Black than We're Painted.
By Proxy.
For Cash Only.
High Spirits.
Sunny Stories.
A Confidential Agent.
A Grape from a Thorn. 12 Illusts.
The Family Scapegrace.
Holiday Tasks.
At Her Mercy.
The Talk of the Town. 12 Illusts.
The Mystery of Mirbridge.
The Word and the Will.
The Burnt Million.
A Trying Patient.
Gwendoline's Harvest.
A Woman's Vengeance.
The Best of Husbands.
The Foster Brothers.
Found Dead.
Kit : A Memory.
Murphy's Master.
Not Wooed but Won.
Married Beneath Him.
Under One Roof.
A Modern Dick Whittington.
With Portrait of Author.

POPULAR EDITIONS, med. 8vo, 9d. net each.
Lost Sir Massingberd.
Walter's Word. | By Proxy.

PEACE ON EARTH : The Story of the Birth of Christ in the Words of the Gospel. Illust. by THOMAS DERRICK. Small 4to, bds., 1s. net.

PENNY (F. E.), Novels by.

Crown 8vo, cloth, 3s. 6d. net each.

The Sanyasi.
Caste and Creed.
Dilys.
The Tea-Planter.
Inevitable Law.
The Rajah.
The Unlucky Mark.
Sacrifice.
Dark Corners.
Love in the Hills.
The Malabar Magician.
The Outcaste.

Crown 8vo, cloth, 6s. net. each.

Love in a Palace.
Love by an Indian River.
Missing!
A Love Tangle.

POPULAR EDITIONS, med. 8vo, 9d. net each.
The Tea-Planter.
Inevitable Law.
Caste and Creed.
The Sanyasi.

PERRIN (ALICE), Novels by.

Crown 8vo, cloth, 3s. 6d. net each.

A Free Solitude. | East of Suez.
The Waters of Destruction.
Red Records.
The Stronger Claim.
Idolatry.

POPULAR EDITIONS, med. 8vo, 9d. net each.
The Stronger Claim.
The Waters of Destruction.
Idolatry. | A Free Solitude.

PETIT HOMME ROUGE (Le).
See under Vizetelly (E. A.), page 31.

PETRARCH'S SECRET ; or, The Soul's Conflict with Passion. Three Dialogues. Translated from the Latin by W. H. DRAPER. With 2 Illustrations. Crown 8vo, cloth, 6s. net.

PHIL MAY'S Sketch-Book : 54 Cartoons. Crown folio, cloth, 2s. 6d. net.

PHIPSON (Dr. T. L.).—Famous Violinists and Fine Violins. Crown 8vo, cloth, 5s. net.

PICKTHALL (MARMADUKE).—
Larkmeadow. Crown 8vo, cl., 6s. net.

PLUTARCH'S Lives of Illus-
trious Men. With Portraits. Two
Vols., 8vo, half-cl., 10s. 6d. net.

POE'S (EDGAR ALLAN) Choice
Works. With an Introduction by CHAS.
BAUDELAIRE. Crown 8vo, cl., 3s. 6d. net.

POLLEN (A. H.).—The Navy in
Battle. Illust. Dy. 8vo, cl., 7s. 6d. net.

POUGIN (ARTHUR).—A Short
History of Russian Music. Translated by LAWRENCE HAWARD. Crown
8vo, cloth, 5s. net.

PRAED (Mrs. CAMPBELL),
Novels by. Crown 8vo, cloth, 3s. 6d.
net each.

Outlaw and Lawmaker.
Christina Chard.
Mrs. Tregaskiss. With 8 Illustrations.
Nulma.
Madame Izan.
The Lost Earl of Ellan.

Our Book of Memories. Letters
from JUSTIN MCCARTHY. With Ports.
and Views. Demy 8vo, cl., 12s. 6d. net.
See also under JUSTIN MCCARTHY.

PRESLAND (JOHN), Dramas
by. Fcap. 4to, cloth, 5s. net each.

Mary Queen of Scots.
Manin and the Defence of Venice.
Marcus Aurelius.
Belisarius, General of the East.
King Monmouth.

Small crown 8vo, cloth, 3s. 6d. net each.

The Deluge, and other Poems.
Songs of Changing Skies.

Lynton and Lynmouth. Illustrated
in Colour by F. J. WIDGERY. Demy 8vo,
cloth, 7s. 6d. net.

PROCTOR (RICHARD A.),
Books by. Cr. 8vo, cloth, 3s. 6d. net each.

Easy Star Lessons. With Star Maps.
Flowers of the Sky. With 55 Illusts.
Familiar Science Studies.

PROCTOR (RICHARD A.)—continued.

Saturn and its System. With 13
Steel Plates. Demy 8vo, cloth. 5s. net.

PRYCE (RICHARD). — Miss
Maxwell's Affections. Cr. 8vo, cl.,
3s. 6d. net.

RAB AND HIS FRIENDS. By
Dr. JOHN BROWN. Square 16mo, with
Frontispiece, cloth, 1s. net.

READE'S (CHARLES) Novels.

Collected LIBRARY EDITION, in Seventeen
Volumes, crown 8vo, cloth, 3s. 6d. net ea.

Peg Woffington; and Christie
Johnstone.
Hard Cash.
The Cloister and the Hearth.
With a Preface by Sir WALTER BESANT.
'It is Never Too Late to Mend.'
The Course of True Love Never
Did Run Smooth; and Single-
heart and Doubleface.
The Autobiography of a Thief;
Jack of all Trades; A Hero and
a Martyr; The Wandering Heir.
Love Me Little, Love Me Long.
The Double Marriage.
Put Yourself in His Place.
A Terrible Temptation.
Griffith Gaunt. | A Woman-Hater.
Foul Play. | A Simpleton.
The Jilt: and Good Stories of Man
and other Animals.
A Perilous Secret.
Readiana; and Bible Characters.

LARGE TYPE, FINE PAPER EDITIONS.

Pott 8vo, cloth, 2s. 6d. net each; leather, gilt
top, 4s. net each.

The Cloister and the Hearth. With
32 Illustrations by M. B. HEWERDINE.

'It is Never Too Late to Mend.'

POPULAR EDITIONS, med. 8vo, 9d. net each.

The Cloister and the Hearth.
'It is Never Too Late to Mend.'
Foul Play. | Hard Cash.
Peg Woffington; and Christie
Johnstone. | Griffith Gaunt.
Put Yourself in His Place.
A Terrible Temptation.
The Double Marriage.
Love Me Little, Love Me Long.
A Perilous Secret.
A Woman-hater.
The Course of True Love.

READE (CHARLES)—*continued.*

The Wandering Heir. LARGE TYPE EDITION, fcap.8vo, cloth, 1s. net.

The Cloister and the Hearth. Illustrations by MATT B. HEWERDINE. Small 4to, cloth 6s. net.—Also Illustrated by BYAM SHAW, R.I. Demy 8vo, cloth, 7s. 6d. net.

REITLINGER (FRÉDÉRIC).—A Diplomat's Memoir of 1870. Translated by HENRY REITLINGER. Cr, 8vo, cloth, 2s. net.

RICHARDSON (Frank), Novels by.

The Man who Lost his Past. With 50 Illustrations by TOM BROWNE, R.I. Crown 8vo, cloth, 3s. 6d. net.

The Bayswater Miracle. Crown 8vo, cloth, 3s. 6d. net,

Crown 8vo, cloth, 6s. net each.
The King's Counsel.
There and Back.

RIDDELL (Mrs.), Novels by.

A Rich Man's Daughter. Crown 8vo, cloth, 3s. 6d. net,

Weird Stories. Crown 8vo, cloth, 3s. 6d. net.

RIVES (AMELIE), Stories by. Crown 8vo, cloth, 3s. 6d. net each.

Barbara Dering.
Meriel: A Love Story.

ROBINSON (F. W.), Novels by. Crown 8vo, cloth, 3s. 6d. net each.
The Hands of Justice.
The Woman in the Dark.

ROLFE (FR.).—Don Tarquinio. Crown 8vo, cloth, 6s. net.

ROLL OF BATTLE ABBEY, THE: List of the Principal Warriors who came from Normandy with William the Conqueror, 1066. In Gold and Colours, 3s. 6d. net.

ROSENGARTEN (A.).—A Hand- book of Architectural Styles. Translated by W. COLLETT-SANDARS. With 630 Illustrations. Cr. 8vo, cloth, 5s. net.

ROSHER (HAROLD). — In the Royal Naval Air Service. With a Preface by ARNOLD BENNETT. Illust. Crown 8vo, 3s. 6d. net. Paper, 1s. net.

ROWLANDS (EFFIE ADE- LAIDE), Novels by. Cr. 8vo, cloth.
The Price Paid. 3s. 6d. net.
Her Husband. 6s. net.

RUSKIN (JOHN).—The King of the Golden River. Square 16mo, with Frontispiece, 1s. net.

Ruskin as a Religious Teacher. By F. W. FARRAR, D.D. Square 16mo, 1s. net.

The Pocket Ruskin. 16mo, cloth, 2s. 6d. net.; leather, gilt top, 4s. net.

RUSSELL (W. CLARK), Novels by. Crown 8vo, cloth, 3s. 6d. net each.

Round the Galley-Fire.
In the Middle Watch.
On the Fo'k'sle Head.
A Book for the Hammock.
The Mystery of the 'Ocean Star.'
The Romance of Jenny Harlowe.
The Tale of the Ten.
An Ocean Tragedy.
My Shipmate Louise.
Alone on a Wide Wide Sea
The Good Ship 'Mohock.'
The Phantom Death.
Is He the Man? | The Last Entry
The Convict Ship. | Heart of Oak.
A Tale of Two Tunnels.
The Death Ship.
Overdue. | Wrong Side Out.

POPULAR EDITIONS, med. 8vo, 9d. net each.

The Convict Ship.
Is He the Man?
My Shipmate Louise.

RUSSELL (DORA), Novels by. Crown 8vo, cloth, 3s. 6d. net each.

A Country Sweetheart.
The Drift of Fate.

RUSSIAN BASTILLE, THE (The Fortress of Schluesselburg). By I. P. YOUVATSHEV. Translated by A. S. RAPPOPORT, M.A. With 16 Plates. Demy 8vo, cloth, 7s. 6d. net.

SAINT AUBYN (ALAN), Novels
by. Crown 8vo, cloth, 3s. 6d. net each.
A Fellow of Trinity. With a Note
by OLIVER WENDELL HOLMES.
The Junior Dean.
Orchard Damerel.
The Master of St. Benedict's.
In the Face of the World.
To His Own Master.
The Tremlett Diamonds.
The Wooing of May.
Fortune's Gate.
A Tragic Honeymoon.
Gallantry Bower.
A Proctor's Wooing.
Bonnie Maggie Lauder.
Mrs. Dunbar's Secret.
Mary Unwin. With 8 Illustrations.

SANDEMAN (GEORGE).—
Agnes. Crown 8vo, cloth, 6s. net.

SAROLEA (CHARLES).—Ger-
man Problems and Personalities.
Crown 8vo, cloth, 5s. net.

SCOTT (CYRIL).—The Celestial
Aftermath. Pott 4to, cloth, 5s. net.
Also LARGE PAPER EDITION limited to
50 Signed Copies, parchment, 21s. net.

SÉLINCOURT (HUGH DE),
Books by.
Oxford from Within. With a Note
and 20 Illustrations in colour and Mono
chrome by YOSHIO MARKINO. Demy 8vo,
cloth, 5s. net.
A Daughter of the Morning.
Crown 8vo, cloth, 6s. net.

SERGEANT (ADELINE), Novels
by. Crown 8vo, cloth, 3s. 6d. net each.
Under False Pretences.
Dr. Endicott's Experiment.
The Missing Elizabeth.

SERMON ON THE MOUNT
(The). Illuminated in Gold and Colours
by ALBERTO SANGORSKI. Fcap. 4to,
Jap. vellum, 3s. 6d. net ; parchment, full
gilt, with silk ties, 6s. net.

ST. MARTIN'S LIBRARY (The).
In pocket size, cloth, 2s. 6d. net per Vol. ;
leather, gilt top, 4s. net per Vol.

By WALTER BESANT.
London. | **Westminster.**
Jerusalem. By BESANT and PALMER.
All Sorts and Conditions of Men.
Sir Richard Whittington.
Gaspard de Coligny.

By GIOVANNI BOCCACCIO.
The Decameron.

By ROBERT BROWNING.
Illustrated in Colours by E. F. BRICKDALE.
Pippa Passes: and **Men and Wo-
men.**
Dramatis Personæ: and **Dra-
matic Romances and Lyrics.**

ST. MARTIN'S LIBRARY—continued.
By ROBERT BUCHANAN.
The Shadow of the Sword.
By HALL CAINE.
The Deemster.
By WILKIE COLLINS.
The Woman in White.
By DANIEL DEFOE.
Robinson Crusoe. With 37 Illus-
trations by G. CRUIKSHANK.
By CHARLES DICKENS.
Speeches. With Portrait
By AUSTIN DOBSON.
Eighteenth Century Vignettes.
In Three Series, each Illustrated.
By W. S. GILBERT.
Original Plays. In Four Series, the
Fourth Series with a Portrait.
By THOMAS HARDY.
Under the Greenwood Tree.
By BRET HARTE.
Condensed Novels.
Mliss, The Luck of Roaring Camp,
and other Stories. With Portrait.
Poetical Works.
By OLIVER WENDELL HOLMES.
**The Autocrat of the Breakfast-
Table.** Illustrated by J. G. THOMSON.
Compiled by A. H. HYATT.
The Charm of London: An Anthology.
The Charm of Edinburgh.
The Charm of Venice.
The Charm of Paris.
By RICHARD JEFFERIES.
The Life of the Fields.
The Open Air.
Nature near London.
By CHARLES LAMB.
The Essays of Elia.
By LORD MACAULAY.
History of England, in 5 Volumes.
By JUSTIN McCARTHY.
The Reign of Queen Anne, in 1 Vol.
**A History of the Four Georges
and of William IV.,** in 2 Vols.
A History of Our Own Times from
Accession of Q. Victoria to 1901, in 4 Vols.
By GEORGE MacDONALD.
Poetical Works. In 2 vols.
Works of Fancy and Imagination
in 10 Vols. 16mo. (For List, see p. 18.)
By W. H. MALLOCK.
The New Republic.
By OUIDA.
Wisdom, Wit, and Pathos.
By CHARLES READE.
The Cloister and the Hearth. With
32 Illustrations by M. B. HEWERDINE.
'It is Never Too Late to Mend.'
By PERCY BYSSHE SHELLEY.
Prose Works. 2 vols., with 2 Ports.
Poetical Works. 2 vols., with 2 Plates.
Selected by FRANK SIDGWICK,
and Illustrated in Colours by BYAM SHAW.
Ballads and Lyrics of Love.
Historical and Legendary Ballads.

ST. MARTIN'S LIBRARY—*continued.*
In pocket size, cloth, 2s. 6d. net per Vol.;
leather, gilt top, 4s. net per Vol.
By ROBERT LOUIS STEVENSON.
An Inland Voyage.
Travels with a Donkey.
The Silverado Squatters.
Memories and Portraits.
Virginibus Puerisque.
Men and Books.
New Arabian Nights.
Across the Plains.
The Merry Men.
Prince Otto.
In the South Seas.
Essays of Travel.
Weir of Hermiston.
Tales and Fantasies.
The Art of Writing.
Lay Morals, etc.   **Poems.**
By H. A. TAINE.
History of English Literature, in
4 Vols. With 32 Portraits.
By TCHEHOV.
Tales. Translated by CONSTANCE GAR-
NETT. Six Vols. Now ready.
By MARK TWAIN.—**Sketches.**
By WALTON and COTTON.
The Complete Angler.
By WALT WHITMAN.
Poems. Selected and Edited by W. M.
ROSSETTI. With Portrait.

SANGORSKI (ALBERTO),
Books Illuminated by. Fcap. 4to.
Jap. vellum 3s. 6d. net each; parchment
gilt, with silk ties, 6s. net each.
Prayers Written at Vailima by
ROBERT LOUIS STEVENSON.
The Sermon on the Mount.
Morte d'Arthur, by LORD TENNYSON.

SCOTT (CYRIL).—The Celestial
Aftermath. Pott 4to, cloth, 5s. net.
LARGE PAPER EDITION, limited to 50
copies, signed by the Author, 21s. net.

SHADOWLESS MAN (THE):
Peter Schlemihl. By A. VON CHAMISSO.
Illustrated by GORDON BROWNE. Demy
8vo, cloth, 2s. net.

SHAKESPEARE LIBRARY
PART I.
The Old-Spelling SHAKESPEARE.
Edited by F. J. FURNIVALL, M.A., D. Litt.,
and F. W. CLARKE, M.A. Demy 8vo, cl.,
2s. 6d. net each Play. Of some of the
plays a Library Edition may be had
at 5s. net each. A list of volumes
on application.

PART II.
The SHAKESPEARE CLASSICS.
Small crown 8vo, quarter-bound antique
grey boards, 2s. 6d. net per vol.; those
marked † may also be had in velvet
persian at 4s. net; and those marked *
on large paper, half parchment, 5s. net.
per vol. Each volume with Frontispiece.
*†1. Lodge's 'Rosalynde': the
original of Shakespeare's 'As
You Like It.' Edited by W. W.
GREG, M.A.   [*Ready.*

SHAKESPEARE LIBRARY—*cont.*

SHAKESPEARE CLASSICS—*cont.*

Volumes published or in preparation.

*†2. Greene's 'Pandosto,' or 'Doras-
tus and Fawnia': the original
of Shakespeare's 'Winter's
Tale.' Ed. by P. G. THOMAS. [*Ready.*

*†3. Brooke's Poem of 'Romeus and
Juliet': the original of Shakespeare's 'Romeo and Juliet.'
Edited by P. A. DANIEL. Modernised
and re-edited by J. J. MUNRO. [*Ready.*

4. 'The Troublesome Reign of
King John': the Play rewritten
by Shakespeare as 'King John.'
Edited by Dr. F. J. FURNIVALL and
JOHN MUNRO, M.A. [*Ready.*

5, 6. 'The History of Hamlet':
With other Documents illustrative of
the sources of Shakspeare's Play, and an
Introductory Study of the LEGEND OF
HAMLET by Prof. I. GOLLANCZ.

*†7. 'The Play of King Leir and His
Three Daughters': the old play
on the subject of King Lear.
Edited by SIDNEY LEE, D.Litt. [*Ready.*

*†8. 'The Taming of a Shrew':
Being the old play used by Shakespeare
in 'The Taming of the Shrew.' Edited
by Professor F. S. BOAS, M.A. [*Ready.*

*†9. The Sources and Analogues of
'A Midsummer Night's Dream.'
Edited by FRANK SIDGWICK. [*Ready.*

10. 'The Famous Victories of
Henry V.'

11. 'The Menæchmi': the original
of Shakespeare's 'Comedy of
Errors.' Latin text, with the Elizabethan Translation. Edited by W. H. D.
ROUSE, Litt.D. [*Ready.*

12. 'Promos and Cassandra':
the source of 'Measure for
Measure.'

13. 'Apolonius and Silla': the
source of 'Twelfth Night.' Edited by
MORTON LUCE. [*Ready.*

14. 'The First Part of the Conten-
tion betwixt the two famous
Houses of York and Lancas-
ter,' and 'The True Tragedy of
Richard, Duke of York': the
originals of the second and third parts of
'King Henry VI.'

15. The Sources of 'The Tempest.'

16. The Sources of 'Cymbeline.'

17. The Sources and Analogues
of 'The Merchant of Venice.'
Edited by Professor I. GOLLANCZ.

18. Romantic Tales: the sources of
'The Two Gentlemen of Verona,' 'Merry
Wives,' 'Much Ado about Nothing,'
'All's Well that Ends Well.'

SHAKESPEARE LIBRARY—*cont.*

*†19, 20. **Shakespeare's Plutarch:** the sources of ' Julius Cæsar,' ' Antony and Cleopatra,' ' Coriolanus,' and ' Timon.' Ed. C. F. TUCKER BROOKE, M.A. [*Ready.*

PART III.

THE LAMB SHAKESPEARE FOR YOUNG PEOPLE.

With Illustrations and Music. Based on MARY AND CHARLES LAMB'S TALES FROM SHAKESPEARE, and edited by Professor I. GOLLANCZ, who has inserted within the prose setting those scenes and passages from the Plays with which the young reader should early become acquainted. The Music arranged by T. MASKELL HARDY. Imperial 16mo, cloth, 1*s.* 6*d.* net per vol. ; leather, 2*s.* 6*d.* net per vol. ; School Edit., linen, 1*s.* net per vol.

   I. **The Tempest.**
  II. **As You Like It.**
 III. **A Midsummer Night's Dream.**
 IV. **The Merchant of Venice.**
  V. **The Winter's Tale.**
 VI. **Twelfth Night.**
VII. **Cymbeline.**
VIII. **Romeo and Juliet.**
 IX. **Macbeth.**
  X. **Much Ado About Nothing.**

 XI. **Life of Shakespeare for the Young.** By Prof. I. GOLLANCZ. [*Preparing.*
XII. **An Evening with Shakespeare:** 10 Dramatic Tableaux for Young People, with Music by T. MASKELL HARDY, and Illustrations. Cloth, 2*s.* net ; leather, 3*s.* 6*d.* net ; linen, 1*s.* 6*d.* net.

PART IV.

SHAKESPEARE'S ENGLAND.

A series of volumes illustrative of the life, thought, and letters of England in the time of Shakespeare.

Robert Laneham's Letter, describing part of the Entertainment given to Queen Elizabeth at Kenilworth Castle in 1575. With Introduction by Dr. FURNIVALL, and Illustrations. Demy 8vo cloth, 5*s.* net.

The Rogues and Vagabonds of Shakespeare's Youth: reprints of Awdeley's 'Fraternitye of Vacabondes,' Harman's 'Caveat for CommonCursetors,' Parson Haben's or Hyberdyne's ' Sermon in Praise of Thieves and Thievery,' &c. With many woodcuts. Edited, with Introduction, by EDWARD VILES and Dr. FURNIVALL. Demy 8vo, cloth, 5*s.* net.

Shakespeare's Holinshed : a reprint of all the passages in Holinshed's 'Chronicle' of which use was made in Shakespeare's Historical Plays, with Notes. Edited by W. G. BOSWELL STONE. Royal 8vo, cloth, 10*s.* 6*d.* net.

SHAKESPEARE LIBRARY—*cont.*

SHAKESPEARE'S ENGLAND—*cont.*

The Shakespeare Allusion Book. Reprints of all references to Shakespeare and his Works before the close of the 17th century, collected by Dr. INGLEBY, Miss L. TOULMIN SMITH, Dr. FURNIVALL, and J. J. MUNRO. Two vols., royal 8vo, cloth, 21*s.* net.

The Book of Elizabethan Verse. Edited with Notes by WILLIAM STANLEY BRAITHWAITE. With Frontispiece and Vignette. Small crown 8vo cloth, 3*s.* 6*d.* net ; vellum gilt, 12*s.* 6*d.* net.

A Study of Shakespeare. By A. C. SWINBURNE. Crown 8vo, cloth, 8*s.*
The Age of Shakespeare. By A. C. SWINBURNE. Cr. 8vo, buckram, 6*s.* net.

SHELLEY'S (PERCY BYSSHE)

Complete Works in VERSE (2 Vols.) and PROSE (2 Vols.), each with Frontispiece. Edited by RICHARD HERNE SHEPHERD. ST. MARTIN'S LIBRARY Edition. Pott 8vo, cloth, 2*s.* 6*d.* net per vol. ; leather gilt, 4*s.* net per vol.

***Also an Edition in 5 vols. cr. 8vo, cloth, 3*s.*6*d.* net per vol., in which the POETICAL WORKS form 3 vols. and the PROSE WORKS 2 vols. *See also* under FLORENCE PRESS BOOKS, page 10.

SHERIDAN'S (RICHARD BRINSLEY) Complete Works

Edited by F. STAINFORTH. With Portrait and Memoir. Cr. 8vo, cloth, 3*s.* 6*d.* net.

SHIEL (M. P.), Novels by.

The Purple Cloud. Crown 8vo, cloth, 3*s.* 6*d.* net.
Unto the Third Generation. Cr. 8vo, cloth, 6*s.* net.

SIGNBOARDS: The History of,

from the Earliest Times ; including Famous Taverns and Remarkable Characters. By JACOB LARWOOD and J. C. HOTTEN. With 95 Illustrations. Crown 8vo, cloth, 3*s.* 6*d.* net.

SIMS (GEORGE R.), Books by.

Crown 8vo, picture cover, 1*s.* net each ; cloth, 1*s.* 6*d.* net each.

The Dagonet Reciter and Reader.
Dagonet Ditties.
Life We Live.
Young Mrs. Caudle.
Li Ting of London.

SIMS (GEORGE R.), Books by—*cont.*
Crown 8vo, cloth, 3s. 6d. net each.

Mary Jane's Memoirs.
Mary Jane Married.
Rogues and Vagabonds.
Anna of the Underworld.
Joyce Pleasantry. With a Frontispiece by HUGH THOMSON.
For Life—and After.
Once upon a Christmas Time. With 8 Illustrations by CHAS. GREEN, R.I.
In London's Heart.
A Blind Marriage.
Without the Limelight.
The Small-part Lady.
Biographs of Babylon.
The Mystery of Mary Anne.
His Wife's Revenge.
Tinkletop's Crime.
Dramas of Life.
Zeph.
Ring o' Bells.
Dagonet Abroad.

POPULAR EDITIONS, med. 8vo, 9d. net each.
Mary Jane's Memoirs.
Mary Jane Married.
Rogues and Vagabonds.

How the Poor Live; and **Horrible London.** Cr. 8vo, leatherette, 1s. net.
Dagonet Dramas. Crown 8vo, 1s. net.

SLADEN (DOUGLAS).—A Japanese Marriage. Med. 8vo, 9d. net.

SLANG DICTIONARY (The): Historical and Anecdotal. Cr. 8vo, cl., 6s. net.

SMEDLEY (CONSTANCE : Mrs. Maxwell Armfield), Novels by.
Crown 8vo, cloth, 3s. 6d. net.
Service. With Frontispiece.

Crown 8vo, cloth, 6s. net. each.

Mothers and Fathers. Frontispiece.
Commoners' Rights. With 8 Illustrations by MAXWELL ARMFIELD.
Una and the Lions.
See also **The Flower Book,** p. 10.

SNAITH (J. C.).—The Coming. Crown 8vo, cloth, 6s. net.

SOMERSET (Lord HENRY).—Songs of Adieu. 4to, Jap. vell., 5s. net.

SPALDING (Kenneth J.). — A Pilgrim's Way. Fcap. 4to, 3s. 6d. net.

SPANISH ISLAM : A History of the Moslems in Spain. By REINHART DOZY. Translated, with Biographical Introduction and additional Notes, by F. G. STOKES. With Frontispiece and Map. Royal 8vo, buckram, 21s. net.

SPEIGHT (E. E.).—The Galleon of Torbay. Crown 8vo, cloth, 6s. net.

SPEIGHT (T. W.), Novels by.
Cr. 8vo, cloth, 3s. 6d. net.

Her Ladyship.
The Grey Monk.
The Master of Trenance.
The Secret of Wyvern Towers.
Doom of Siva.
As it was Written
The Web of Fate.
Experiences of Mr. Verschoyle.
Stepping Blindfold.

SPIELMANN (MRS. M. H.), Books by.

Margery Redford and her Friends. With Illustrations by GORDON BROWNE. Large crown 8vo, cloth, 5s. net.

The Rainbow Book: Sixteen Tales of Fun and Fancy. With 37 Illustrations by ARTHUR RACKHAM, HUGH THOMSON and other artists. Large crown 8vo, cloth, 2s. 6d. net.

'SPY' (FORTY YEARS OF), by LESLIE WARD. With over 150 Illustrations after Portraits and Caricatures by the Author. Demy 8vo, cloth, 7s. 6d. net.

STATHAM (H. HEATHCOTE). —What is Music? With Frontispiece. Crown 8vo, cloth, 3s. 6d. net.

STEDMAN (E. C.).—Victorian Poets. Crown 8vo, cloth, 9s. net.

STERNE (LAURENCE).— A Sentimental Journey. With 89 Illustrations by T. H. ROBINSON, and Portrait. Cr. 8vo, cloth, 3s. 6d. net; post 8vo, cloth, 2s. 6d. net; leather, 4s. net.

STEVENSON (R. LOUIS), Works by.

Virginibus Puerisque, and other Papers. FLORENCE PRESS EDITION. With 12 Illustrations in Coloured Collotype by NORMAN WILKINSON. Cr. 4to. bds., £2 12s. 6d. net; vellum, £3 3s. net.

Stevenson's Poems: Complete Edition. Printed in the Florence Type. Small fcap. 4to, gilt top, 12s. 6d. net.

Crown 8vo, buckram. 6s. net each.

Travels with a Donkey. With a Frontispiece by WALTER CRANE.
An Inland Voyage. With a Frontispiece by WALTER CRANE.
Familiar Studies of Men & Books.
The Silverado Squatters.
New Arabian Nights.
The Merry Men. | Lay Morals, &c.
Underwoods: Poems.
Memories and Portraits.
Virginibus Puerisque. | Ballads.
Songs of Travel.
Prince Otto. | Across the Plains.
Weir of Hermiston.
In the South Seas.
Essays of Travel.
Tales and Fantasies.
Essays in the Art of Writing.
Records of a Family of Engineers

The above books are also issued in a FINE PAPER EDITION, pott 8vo, cloth, 2s. 6d. net each; leather, 4s. net, with the exception of 'Underwoods' and 'Ballads,' which are printed in 1 vol. together with 'Songs of Travel,' under the title of 'Poems.' 'Records of a Family of Engineers' is published at 6s. net only.

A Lowden Sabbath Morn. With Coloured Front. and numerous Illus. by A. S. BOYD. Cr. 8vo, buckram, 5s. net.

Large crown 8vo, cloth, 5s. net each; parchment, 7s. 6d. net each; or, LARGE PAPER EDITIONS, vel., 12s. 6d. net each.

An Inland Voyage. Illustrated in Colour by NOEL ROOKE.
Travels with a Donkey in the Cevennes Illustrated in Colour by NOEL ROOKE.
A Child's Garden of Verses. Illustrated in Colour by MILLICENT SOWERBY. Large crown 8vo, cloth, 6s. net; LARGE PAPER ED., parchmt., 10s. 6d. net.

Long fcap. 8vo, quarter-cloth, 1s. net each.
Father Damien.
Talk and Talkers.

A Christmas Sermon. Post 8vo, bds., 1s. net; leather, 2s. net. Also a MINIATURE EDITION in velvet calf, 2s. net.

Prayers Written at Vailima. Post 8vo, bds., 1s. net; leather, 2s. net. Also a MINIATURE EDITION in velvet calf yapp, 2s. net; and the EDITION DE LUXE, Illum. by A. SANGORSKI in gold and colours, fcap. 4to. Jap. vel., gilt top 3s. 6d. net.; parch. gilt, with ties, 6s. net.

STEVENSON (R. L.)—continued.
New Arabian Nights. POPULAR EDITION. medium 8vo, 9d. net.
The Suicide Club; and The Rajah's Diamond. (From NEW ARABIAN NIGHTS.) With 8 Illustrations by W. J. HENNESSY. Crown 8vo, cloth, 3s. 6d. net.

16mo, decorated cloth, 1s. net each.
The Sire de Malétroit's Door.
A Lodging for the Night.
The Waif Woman.
On the Choice of a Profession.

The Pavilion on the Links. With Illustrations by GORDON BROWNE, R.I. Demy 8vo, cloth, 2s. net.
The Stevenson Reader. Post 8vo, cl., 2s. 6d. net; buckram, gilt top, 3s. 6d. net; SCHOOL EDITION, cloth, 1s. 6d. net.
The Pocket R.L.S.: Favourite Passages. 16mo, cl., 2s. 6d. net; leather, 4s. net.
Brave Words about Death. Selected from the Writings of Stevenson. Pott 8vo, decorated cover, 1s. net.
R. L. Stevenson: A Study. By H. B. BAILDON. Crown 8vo, buckram, 5s. net.
Recollections of R. L. Stevenson in the Pacific. By ARTHUR JOHNSTONE. Cr. 8vo, buckram, 6s. net.

STOCKTON (FRANK R.).—The Young Master of Hyson Hall. With 36 Illustrations. Crown 8vo, cloth, 3s. 6d. net.

STOKES (FRANCIS GRIFFIN), Translated and Edited by:
Epistolæ Obscurorum Virorum. The Latin text with English Rendering. Roya 8vo, buckram, 25s. net.
Spanish Islam: a History of the Moslems in Spain. By REINHART DOZY. Royal 8vo, buckram. 21s. net.

STONE (CHRISTOPHER), Novels by. Cr. 8vo, cloth, 6s. net each.
They also Serve.
The Shoe of a Horse.
The Noise of Life. 3s. 6d. net.

STOTT (BEATRICE).—Christian Derrick. Crown 8vo, cloth, 6s. net.

STRACHEY (LYTTON).—Eminent Victorians. With 6 Portraits. Demy 8vo, cloth, 10s. 6d. net.

STRAUS (RALPH), Novels by. Crown 8vo, cloth, 6s. net each.
The Man Apart
The Little God's Drum.

STRUTT (JOSEPH). — The Sports and Pastimes of the People of England. With 140 Illustrations. Crown 8vo, cloth, 3s. 6d. net.

STUART (H. LONGAN), Novels by. Crown 8vo, cloth, 6s. net each.
Weeping Cross. | Fenella.

STUCKENBERG (VIGGO).—By the Wayside. Translated from the Danish and illustrated by Una Hook. Small fcap. 4to, boards, 3s. 6d. net.

SUTRO (ALFRED). — The Foolish Virgins. Fcp. 8vo, cloth, 1s. 6d. net.

SWIFT'S (Dean) Choice Works, in Prose and Verse. Cr. 8vo, cl., 3s. 6d. net.
Jonathan Swift: A Study. By J. CHURTON COLLINS. Cr. 8vo, cl., 3s. 6d. net.

SWINBURNE'S (ALGERNON CHARLES) Works.

Mr. Swinburne's Collected Tragedies. In 5 Vols., cr. 8vo, 30s. net the set.

Songs before Sunrise. FLORENCE PRESS EDITION. Crown 4to, hand-made paper, boards, 26s. net ; vellum, 36s. net.

Selections. Fcap. 8vo, cloth, 6s.

Dolores. Small 4to, boards, 1s. net.

The Queen-Mother; and Rosamond. Crown 8vo, 7s. 6d. net.
Atalanta in Calydon. Crown 8vo, 6s.
Chastelard: A Tragedy. Crown 8vo, 7s.
Poems and Ballads. FIRST SERIES Crown 8vo, 9s.
Poems and Ballads. SECOND SERIES Crown 8vo, 9s.
Poems and Ballads. THIRD SERIES Crown 8vo, 7s.
Songs before Sunrise. Cr. 8vo, 10s. 6d
Bothwell: A Tragedy. Crown 8vo, 12s. 6d.
Songs of Two Nations. Crown 8vo, 6s.
George Chapman (In Vol. II. of G CHAPMAN'S Works.) Cr. 8vo, 3s. 6d. net.
Essays and Studies. Crown 8vo, 12s.
Erechtheus: A Tragedy. Crown 8vo, 6s.
A Note on Charlotte Bronte. Crown 8vo, 6s.
A Study of Shakespeare. Cr. 8vo, 8s.
Songs of the Springtides. Cr. 8vo, 6s.
Studies in Song. Crown 8vo, 7s.
Mary Stuart: A Tragedy. Crown 8vo, 8s.
Tristram of Lyonesse. Crown 8vo, 9s.
A Century of Roundels. Cr. 8vo, 6s.
A Midsummer Holiday. Cr. 8vo, 7s.
Marino Faliero: A Tragedy. Cr. 8vo, 6s.
A Study of Victor Hugo. Cr. 8vo, 6s.
Miscellanies. Crown 8vo, 12s.
Locrine: A Tragedy. Crown 8vo, 6s.
A Study of Ben Jonson. Cr. 8vo, 7s.
The Sisters: A Tragedy. Crown 8vo, 6s.
Astrophel, &c. Crown 8vo, 7s.
Studies in Prose and Poetry. Crown 8vo, 9s.
The Tale of Balen. Crown 8vo, 7s.
Rosamund, Queen of the Lombards: A Tragedy. Crown 8vo, 6s.
A Channel Passage. Crown 8vo, 7s.
Love's Cross-Currents: A Year's Letters. Crown 8vo, 6s. net.
William Blake. Crown 8vo, 6s. net.

SWINBURNE (ALGERNON CHARLES) —continued.
The Duke of Gandia. Crown 8vo, 5s.
The Age of Shakespeare. Crown 8vo, 6s. net.
Charles Dickens. Cr. 8vo, 3s. 6d. net.

SWINNERTON (FRANK), Novels by.
The Young Idea. | The Casement. The Merry Heart. 3s. 6d. net ea.

SYRETT (NETTA), Novels by. Crown 8vo, cloth, 3s. 6d. net each.
Anne Page.
A Castle of Dreams.
Olivia L. Carew.

Crown 8vo, cloth, 6s. net each.
Drender's Daughter.
The Endless Journey, &c.
Three Women.
Barbara of the Thorn.

Troublers of the Peace. 5s. net.

POPULAR EDITIONS, medium 8vo, 9d. net.
Anne Page. | Olivia L. Carew. Three Women.

TAINE'S History of English Literature. Trans. by HENRY VAN LAUN. Four Vols., with 32 Portraits, pott 8vo, cloth, 2s. 6d. net each ; leather, gilt top, 4s. net each.

TCHEHOV (ANTON).—Tales translated from the Russian by Constance Garnett. Six vols. now ready. I. The Darling, etc. II. The Duel, etc. III. The Lady with the Dog, etc. IV. The Party, etc. V. The Wife, etc. VI. The Witch, etc. Pott 8vo cloth, 2s. 6d. net; leather, 4s. net each.

TENNYSON (CHARLES).— Cambridge from Within. Illusts. by HARRY MORLEY. Dy. 8vo, cl., 5s. net.

THACKERAY(W. M.).—The Rose and The Ring. Illusts. by GORDON BROWNE. Demy 8vo, cloth, 3s. 6d. net.
The Pocket Thackeray. Arranged by A. H. HYATT. 16mo, cloth, 2s. 6d. net; leather, gilt top, 4s. net.

THOMPSON (FRANCIS). The Hound of Heaven. Ten Drawings Illustrating by FRIDESWITH HUDDART. Royal 4to, boards, 7s. 6d. net. Also 50 copies on parchment.

THOREAU: His Life and Aims. By H. A. PAGE. Post 8vo, buckram, 3s. 6d. net.

TIMBS (JOHN), Works by. Crown 8vo, cloth, 3s. 6d. net each.
Clubs and Club Life in London. With 41 Illustrations.
English Eccentrics and Eccentricities. With 48 Illustrations.

TROLLOPE (ANTHONY), Novels by.
Crown 8vo, cloth, 3s. 6d. net each.

The Way We Live Now.
Frau Frohmann. | **Marion Fay.**
The Land-Leaguers.
Mr. Scarborough's Family.
John Caldigate.

TURKISH ENIGMA, The.
Translated from the French by WINIFRED STEPHENS. Crown 8vo, cloth, 5s. net.

TWAIN'S (MARK) Books.
UNIFORM LIBRARY EDITION. Crown 8vo, cloth, 4s. 6d. net each.

Mark Twain's Library of Humour
With 197 Illustrations by E. W. KEMBLE.
Roughing It: and The Innocents at Home. With 200 Illustrations by F. A. FRASER.
The American Claimant. With 81 Illustrations by HAL HURST and others.
Pudd'nhead Wilson. With Portrait and Six Illustrations by LOUIS LOEB.
* **The Adventures of Tom Sawyer.** With 111 Illustrations.
Tom Sawyer Abroad. With 26 Illustrations by DAN BEARD.
Tom Sawyer, Detective. With Port.
* **A Tramp Abroad.** With 314 Illusts.
* **The Innocents Abroad; and The New Pilgrim's Progress.** With 234 Illusts. (The 2s. 6d. edition is also known as MARK TWAIN'S PLEASURE TRIP.)
* **The Gilded Age.** By MARK TWAIN and C. D. WARNER. With 212 Illusts.
* **The Prince and the Pauper.** With 190 Illustrations.
* **Life on the Mississippi.** 300 Illusts.
* **The Adventures of Huckleberry Finn.** 174 Illusts. by E. W. KEMBLE.
* **A Yankee at the Court of King Arthur.** 220 Illusts. by DAN BEARD.
* **The Stolen White Elephant.**
* **The £1,000,000 Bank-Note.**
A Double-barrelled Detective Story. With 7 Illustrations.
Personal Recollections of Joan of Arc. With 12 Illusts. by F. V. DU MOND.
More Tramps Abroad.
The Man that Corrupted Hadleyburg. With Frontispiece.
The Choice Works of Mark Twain. With Life, Portrait, and Illustrations.
** The Books marked * may be had in post 8vo, cl., without Illustrations, at 2s. 6d. net each.

POPULAR EDITIONS, medium 8vo, 9d. net each.

Tom Sawyer. | **A Tramp Abroad.**
The Prince and the Pauper.
Huckleberry Finn.

Mark Twain's Sketches. Pott 8vo, cloth, 2s 6d. net; leather, gilt top, 4s. net; post 8vo, cloth, 2s. 6d. net.
Mark Twain's Letters. Two vols. Demy 8vo, cloth, 18s. net.

TYTLER (SARAH), Novels by.
Crown 8vo, cloth, 3s. 6d. net each.

Buried Diamonds.
The Blackhall Ghosts.
What She Came Through.
The Macdonald Lass.
The Witch-Wife.
Rachel Langton.
Sapphira.
Mrs. Carmichael's Goddesses.
A Honeymoon's Eclipse.
A Young Dragon.
Three Men of Mark.
In Clarissa's Day.
Sir David's Visitors.
The Poet and His Guardian Angel.

UPWARD (ALLEN), Novels by.
The Queen against Owen. Crown 8vo, cl., 3s. 6d. net.
The Phantom Torpedo-Boats. Crown 8vo, cloth, 3s. 6d. net.

VAN VORST (MARIE).—Fairfax
and his Pride. Crown 8vo, cloth, 6s. net.

VICENZA (The PAINTERS of).
By TANCRED BORENIUS. With 15 full-page Plates. Demy 8vo, cloth, 7s. 6d. net.

VIOLIN TONE. By HIDALGO MOYA
and TOWRY PIPER. Cr. 8vo, cl., 5s. net.

VIZETELLY (ERNEST A.), Books by.
A Path of Thorns: Cr. 8vo, cloth 6s. net.

My Days of Adventure: the Fall of France, 1870-71. With a Frontisp. Demy 8vo, cloth, 7s. 6d. net.

The True Story of Alsace-Lorraine. With Map. Demy 8vo, cloth, 10s. 6d. net.

The Court of the Tuileries, 1852. 1870. Demy 8vo, cloth, 5s. net.

My Adventures in the Commune. Demy 8vo, cl., 12s 6d. net.

In Seven Lands. Demy 8vo, cloth 12s. 6d. net.

WALTON and COTTON'S
Complete Angler. Pott 8vo, cloth, 2s. 6d. net; leather, gilt top, 4s. net.

WARDEN (FLORENCE), by.

Crown 8vo, cloth. 3s. 6d. net each.

Joan, the Curate.
The Heart of a Girl. With 8 Illusts.
Tom Dawson.
The Youngest Miss Brown.
A Fight to a Finish.
The Old House at the Corner.
Love and Lordship
What Ought She to Do?
My Lady of Whims.

Tom Dawson. Medium 8vo, 9d. net.

WARRANT to Execute Charles I.

With the 59 Signatures and Seals. 2s. net.
Warrant to Execute Mary Queen of Scots. 2s. net.

WESTALL (WILL.), Novels by.

Crown 8vo, cloth, 3s. 6d. net each.

Trust-Money.
A Woman Tempted Him.
For Honour and Life.
Her Two Millions.
Two Pinches of Snuff.
With the Red Eagle.
A Red Bridal. | Nigel Fortescue.
Ben Clough. | Birch Dene.
Sons of Belial. | Strange Crimes.
Her Ladyship's Secret.
The Phantom City.
Ralph Norbreck's Trust.
A Queer Race. | Red Ryvington.
Roy of Roy's Court.
As Luck would have it.
As a Man Sows. | The Old Bank.
Dr. Wynne's Revenge.
The Sacred Crescents.
A Very Queer Business.

With the Red Eagle. Med. 8vo, 9d. net.

WHISHAW (FRED.), Novels

by. Crown 8vo, cloth, 3s. 6d. net each.
A Forbidden Name. | Mazeppa.
Many Ways of Love. With 8 Illusts.
Near the Tsar, near Death.

WHITMAN (WALT), Poems by.

Selected by W. M. Rossetti. Pott 4to, cloth, 2s. 6d. net ; leather, 4s. net.
Drum Taps. Special War Edition. Small 4to ; decorated cover, 1s. net.

WILDE (LADY).—The Ancient

Legends, Charms, and Superstitions of Ireland. Cr. 8vo, cloth, 3s. 6d. net.

WILLIAMS (W. MATTIEU).—

The Chemistry of Cookery. Crown 8vo, cloth, 5s. net.

WILSON (Dr. ANDREW), by.

Leisure-Time Studies. With Illustrations. Crown 8vo, cloth. 5s. net.

Common Accidents, and how to Treat Them. Cr. 8vo, cloth, 1s. net ; paper cover, 6d. net.

WOLSELEY (LADY).—Women

and the Land. Cr. 8vo, cloth, 5s. net.

WRAGGE (CLEMENT L.).—

The Romance of the South Seas. With 84 Illusts. Cr. 8vo, cl., 6s. net.

WRAY (ROGER).—Madcaps and

Madmen. Crown 8vo, cloth, 5s. net.

ZOLA (ÉMILE), Novels by.

UNIFORM EDITION. Mostly Translated or Edited, with Introductions, by ERNEST A. VIZETELLY. Cr. 8vo, cl., 3s. 6d. net each.

His Masterpiece. | The Joy of Life.
Germinal. | Thérèse Raquin
The Honour of the Army.
Abbé Mouret's Transgression.
The Fortune of the Rougons.
The Conquest of Plassans.
The Dram-Shop.
The Fat and the Thin. | Money.
His Excellency. | The Dream.
The Downfall. | Doctor Pascal.
Lourdes. | Fruitfulness.
Rome. | Work.
Paris. | Truth.

The Downfall. WAR EDITION. Cr. 8vo. cloth, 2s. net.
POPULAR EDITIONS, medium 8vo, 9d. net each.

Abbé Mouret's Transgression.
The Fortune of the Rougons.
Lourdes | Rome. | The Downfall.
Paris. | Money. | The Dram-
The Joy of Life. | shop.
Germinal. | Thérèse Raquin.
Dr. Pascal.

UNWIN BROTHERS, LIMITED, THE GRESHAM PRESS, WOKING AND LONDON.